D0167571

CARD GAMES
AROUND THE WORLD

Sid Sackson

DOVER PUBLICATIONS, INC.
New York

Bibliographical Note

This Dover edition, first published in 1994, is an unabridged republication of the work first published by Prentice-Hall, Inc., Englewood Cliffs, New Jersey, in 1981 under the title *Playing Cards Around the World*.

Library of Congress Cataloging-in-Publication Data

Sackson, Sid.
    [Playing cards around the world]
    Card games around the world / Sid Sackson.
        p.   cm.
    Originally published: Playing cards around the world. Englewood Cliffs, N.J. : Prentice-Hall, © 1981.
    ISBN 0-486-28100-0 (pbk.)
    1. Card games. I. Title.
GV1243.S23   1994
795.4—dc20   94-18073
                                          CIP

Manufactured in the United States of America
Dover Publications, Inc., 31 East 2nd Street, Mineola, N.Y. 11501

Table of Contents

This book is dedicated to all these wonderful people who helped it take shape: Audrey and Ronnie Corn and their son Jordan, Barbara and Dave Horn, Annette and Phil Laurence and their daughter Jill, Anne and Claude Soucie ... and BB, my wife and constant helpmate. And special thanks to Michael Dummett, whose patient research led me to so many of the Asian card games.

Introduction

For hundreds of years and in almost every corner of the world, people have played with little pieces of cardboard or thin wood or even ivory—all of which we call cards. Africa is the one major corner of the world that never developed an interest in cards. Instead, Africans have been fascinated by games using pebbles or nuts which are moved through a series of holes scooped in the ground or carved in wood. These, like cards, vary from games in which luck determines everything to games in which the outcome depends solely on the players' skill.

It is surprising how little is known about the history of cards. Most authorities agree that cards were first used in China more than eight hundred years ago. There seem to have been three kinds of decks: One deck had the different possible throws of two dice, another contained cards representing the pieces of the Chinese chess game, and the third was based on (or possibly interchangeable with) the paper money of that time and seems to be the ancestor of today's cards.

As the Chinese moved to other areas of the Far East they brought their cards with them. Japanese cards, however, are completely different and may have been introduced by Portuguese sailors when they first began to trade with the island empire. Indian cards, too, are different—they are round and contain eight or ten suits (an explanation of suit is given in the next chapter) of twelve cards each.

How cards came to Europe is anybody's guess. Some historians say that the Gypsies brought them; others say that the

Crusaders came back from the Holy Land with spices and cards; some claim it was the Venetian traders; and still others insist they were brought by the Moors who conquered almost all of Spain.

Once cards hit Europe they were a runaway success. All of a sudden from all corners there are references to the games that were played and the decks used to play them. Probably the earliest deck was the Tarot. This consisted of four suits of fourteen cards each—a king, queen, chevalier, jack, and the numbers from 10 to 1; added to these were twenty-two "trumps," with all kinds of fanciful names and pictures and numbered with Roman numerals from XXII to I.

Surprisingly, as time went by the games tended to become simpler rather than more complicated, and decks became simpler too. In France the trumps and the chevaliers were dropped, leaving a deck of fifty-two cards. This deck was carried to England and then to the colonies in the new world. It is now known almost everywhere in the world. In other areas even smaller decks were formed—possibly due to limits set by the printing presses or the size of pasteboard sheets available. In Italy a forty-card deck became common—with a king, queen, jack, 7, 6, 5, 4, 3, 2, ace in each suit. Spain used either the forty-card deck or one of forty-eight cards without a 10, in each case keeping the chevalier instead of the queen. Germany went for a thirty-six card deck—with a king, queen, chevalier, jack, 10, 9, 8, 7, ace; often the chevaliers were also dropped, leaving thirty-two cards.

You may be wondering what an "ace" is. Well, it is really a one, the name coming from the Latin (*as*) and the Greek (*heis*) word for a unit. As a one it should be the lowest card in the deck, but in most games it is at the top. No one knows for sure why this puzzling switch occurred. Some authorities say it happened at the time of the American or the French Revolution, when common people rose to positions of authority at the top. But, logical as this may seem, aces were on top long before this.

In choosing the games to include in this book I have tried to meet three goals:

1. *Provide games from as many different geographic areas as possible.* You will see that most of the games are associated with a given country. To the best of my knowledge this is either the country in which it originated or where it became the "national" game. But I won't be too surprised if supporters of other countries' claims disagree.

2. *Include all of the major games.* With the help of this book you will become acquainted with the various card games; you will understand the games your parents play; and, of course, you will learn to play them yourself.

3. *Include games that are fun to play*—for the reader and the whole family.

Some games, such as Blackjack, Whist, Cribbage, Contract Bridge, Canasta, have fixed rules that everyone follows. Other games are more relaxed, and players tend to make their own "house rules"; just be sure that all players know what they are before beginning to play. The older the game, the more variations there are. I have tried to provide the rules that I think are the most fun to play. The information I found on most of the Asian games was so sketchy that I practically had to develop new games. But I was careful to use all the information I did have.

Before getting to the games themselves, I will explain a number of terms and ways of doing things that are common to many (or sometimes all) card games. So if, later on, you come across something that may not be completely described, just take a quick look back at Chapter 1.

1
Card Game Terms

The terms described below are common to many card games. When something is done differently in a certain game, the differences will be clearly spelled out.

The Cards A "regular" deck consists of 52 cards, divided into 4 equal "suits." The suits are spades (♠), hearts (♡), diamonds (♢), and clubs (♣). Each suit contains 13 "ranks"—ace (A), king (K), queen (Q), jack (J), 10, 9, 8, 7, 6, 5, 4, 3, and 2. This is the "regular" order of the ranks—with ace the highest. Often there are other orders, and sometimes the order doesn't matter at all.

Kings, queens, and jacks are called "picture" cards. The others are called "number" cards.

Regular decks come with two extra cards, called "jokers" (undoubtedly derived from "the fool"—one of the trumps in the Tarot deck). These belong to no suit and no rank and in certain games have special uses.

Shuffle and Cut To "shuffle" the deck means to mix the cards thoroughly so their order is changed. You'll have to ask someone how to do this, since it is just about impossible to describe in words.

After the deck is shuffled, it is often "cut" (one reason is to change the bottom card in case it is accidentally exposed during shuffling). The deck is placed face down on the table. A player lifts about half of the cards, puts them on the table, and then places the bottom half on top.

Players can also cut to see who will be the first to "deal," or distribute the cards. Each player lifts a part of the deck, announces the bottom card, and then replaces the cards on the deck. The player cutting the highest card is the first dealer.

Another use for cutting is to divide the players into partnerships (as described in the games where it is used).

Direction of Dealing, Play, etc. Unless otherwise noted, the direction used is always clockwise. A player dealing starts by giving a card or cards to the player on his left and continues around to the left. The play during a "hand" similarly rotates to the left. When, in the course of a game, there is more than one deal, each new dealer is the player to the left of the one who dealt the last hand.

Deal "To deal" means to pass out cards from the deck to the players. "A deal" means everything that happens from the time the cards are passed out until the end of the play with these cards.

Hand "Hand" is the term for the cards a player holds in his hand before they are played. In some games cards can be placed on the table in front of a player and still remain a part of his hand. "A hand" is also used to mean the same as "a deal."

Trick-taking Games A large family of games is based on this type of play. The following are some of the terms you'll need to know.

A "trick" is one card played, in turn, by each player to the table. The trick is won by the player playing the most powerful card.

In some games one suit is chosen as a "trump." The other suits are "plain" suits. Any card of a trump suit is more powerful than any card of a plain suit.

The "lead" is the first card played to a trick.

To "follow suit" is to play a card of the same suit as the card that was led.

Chips Many of the games call for the use of "chips." These can be found in various sizes, but the size doesn't matter. They usually come in three colors: white, which have a point value of 1; red, which have a point value of 5; and blue, which have a point value of 10.

If chips are not available, substitutes can be used—such as

play money from a board game, buttons, squares cut from heavy cardboard, or anything else you can think of.

In some games chips are gathered into "pools" (also known as "pots") which are won according to the rules of the game. An amount of chips placed into a pool before each deal is called an "ante."

Other Terms You will find many other terms that are explained with the games in which they are used. Some have rather strange names that don't necessarily explain their origins.

For example, "schneider" and "schwarz" are used in a number of games. The first means to beat the opponent badly; the second means to beat him even worse. In German schneider means tailor, and schwarz means black. I never was able to find any explanation for their use in the games.

2
Games from Asia

SAMPEN (sam' pan) from China.

Number of players 2 to 11.

Difficulty level Easy to learn and to play—a fast-moving game that is mainly a matter of luck.

Object To get rid of your cards.

The Deck You'll need the following 30 cards from each of two regular 52-card decks—the A, 2, 3, 4, 5, 6, 7, 8, 9 of spades, hearts, and diamonds; the J, Q, and K of clubs. You should have 60 cards.

The Deal Five cards are dealt to each player. The dealer then places the remainder of the deck face down in the center of the table and turns the top card face up next to the deck.

The Play If any player has the exact same card as the face-up card, he places it on top. The player then chooses any card from his hand and places it face up on the pile. *For example, the first card turned is the ♡3. Betty has the other ♡3 in her hand and plays it. She then puts the ♣Q on the pile.*

As each new card is placed on the pile, any player with the identical card plays it. If no player has the identical card, the dealer turns the top card from the deck face up.

Continue in this manner until one player plays his last card. This player is the winner.

The winner deals for the next game.

Variation The game is more challenging if more cards are dealt to the players. The following are the maximum number that should be dealt, depending on how many are playing.

NUMBER OF PLAYERS	NUMBER OF CARDS
2–3	15
4	13
5	11
6	9
7–8	7

CHA KAU TSZ' (cha cow' tsu) from China.

Number of players 2 to 4.

Difficulty level Medium—it's a little tricky to catch on.

Object To win a certain number of tricks.

The Deck Use the same deck as that used for Sampen. An A is a 1, the lowest card in a suit. A picture card is also considered a 1, but in a very special way, as will be explained later.

Chips Chips are needed for keeping score. Give each player 10 white, 5 red, and 5 blue.

The Deal If 3 or 4 are playing, 14 cards are dealt to each—2 at a time. If 2 are playing, 15 cards are dealt to each—3 at a time.

The Play The player to the left of the dealer starts by leading one of the following: 1. any single card; 2. a sequence of three or more cards of the same suit (such as ♠A-♠2-♠3 or ◇5-◇6-◇7-◇8); 3. a group of three or more cards of the same rank, including each of the three suits. *For example, ◇4-♠4-♡4 or ◇2-◇2-♠2-♡2 are OK to lead; but ♠7-♠7-♡7-♡7 are not.* If a player has an A of each suit, he can also add as many pictures as desired when leading. (The seven cards shown could all be led together.)

Each player in turn plays as many cards as were led. Any card or cards may be played, but in order to win the trick or tricks a player must do the following:

1. If a number card is led, the highest card of that suit played wins the trick; with two equal cards, the first to be played wins. If a picture is led, the first number card played sets the suit for that trick; if all players throw pictures, the player leading wins the trick.

2. Any higher sequence of the same length, regardless of suit, wins the tricks. *For example, in a 4-player game George leads ♠2-♠3-♠4. Helen has a sequence of ♡A-♡2-♡3-♡4 in her hand; since her 2-3-4 would not beat George's, she plays three other cards instead. Irma plays ♠4-♠5-♠6. John wins the tricks with ◇5-◇6-◇7.*

3. The group of the highest rank wins the tricks, but remember that each of the three suits must be included in a group.

The player winning a sequence or a group is credited with as many tricks as the number of cards led. The player winning the trick or tricks leads next, until all of the cards have been played.

Scoring Each player counts the number of tricks he has won. All players except the one with the most tricks must pay chips into a pool in the center of the table. The number of points paid is the difference between the most tricks won in that hand and the number won by the player paying. *For example, George ends up with 3 tricks, Helen has 6, Irma has 0, and John has 5. George pays 3 points, Irma pays 6 points, and John pays 1. As another example, George, Helen, and Irma all end up with 4 tricks, while John gets 2; John pays 2 points.*

Winning the Pool New hands are played, the chance to deal rotating to the left, until one player succeeds in winning the number of tricks shown in the table below. After the other players pay to the pool in the usual manner, that player takes all the chips in the pool.

NUMBER OF PLAYERS	TRICKS TO WIN POOL
4	8 or more
3	9 or more
2	11 or more

The game can end when a pool is won, or the players can agree to continue playing for another pool. When the game is ended, the player with the most points in chips is the winner.

KHANHOO   from China, but was also quite popular in England about a hundred years ago. It could very possibly be the ancestor of all the Rummy games that we now play.

Number of players   2 to 4.

Difficulty level   Hard—you have to keep track of a lot of cards.

Object   To go out by arranging all the cards in your hand into certain combinations, or "melds."

The Deck   Use the same deck as that used for Sampen and add one joker. An A is a 1, the lowest card in a suit. Pictures are combined with other cards in special ways as explained under Melds.

The Game for 2 or 3 Players   This will be described first, followed by the differences in the game for 4 players.

The Deal   The dealer deals 15 cards to all players—3 at a time—and then finally 1 more card to the player on his left. The remainder of the cards are placed face down in the center of the table as a drawing deck.

Melds   The following are the different ways in which the cards can be arranged in melds, with the point value of each type of meld.

	POINTS
1. *Sequence* 3 or more cards of the same suit in numerical order	1
2. *Aces* any 3 aces, not necessarily of different suits	1
3. *Triplet* 3 cards of the same rank— from 2 through 9—1 of each suit	2
4. *Royal assembly* ♣K-♣Q-♣J	3
5. *Court melds* a) ♣K-♡9-♡9	4
b) ♣Q-♠8-♠8	4
c) ♣J-◊7-◊7	4
6. *Khanhoo* ♡A-♠2-◊3	5
7. *Double aces* 2 melds of aces	10
8. *Double triplet* 2 triplets of the same rank	10
9. *Double royal* 2 royal assemblies	10
10. *Double khanhoo* 2 khanhoos	15

7

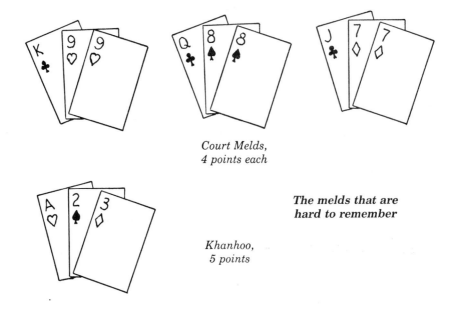

Court Melds,
4 points each

The melds that are
hard to remember

Khanhoo,
5 points

The player who gets the joker can use it to represent any card in forming a meld.

The Play The player with 16 cards discards one face up next to the drawing deck. Each player, in turn, may take the top card from the discard pile or the top card from the drawing deck. He then discards one card.

When three play, a player may sometimes be able to claim the top discard out of turn. This is called "bumping" and is explained later.

If the drawing deck runs out, take all the cards in the discard pile except the top one, shuffle them, and place them face down to form a new drawing deck.

Bumping A player may claim a discard out of turn if the card is immediately used in any meld except a sequence. The two cards from his hand are added to the new card and kept face up before the player. The meld cannot be changed in any way after it is formed.

If the player whose turn it is also wants to use the card in a meld other than a sequence, he announces this. The player able to form the more valuable meld gets the card. If both are equally valuable, the player whose turn it is gets the preference.

For example, Alice discards the ♠2 and Carl claims it. Betty whose turn it is also wants it. If Carl wants it for a khanhoo and Betty only for a triplet of 2's, Carl gets the card. If both, however, want it for a triplet, Betty wins.

After bumping, the player makes a discard and play continues to his left.

Going Out When, after picking up a card, a player is able to form 15 cards into melds, the player announces this while discarding and the play ends. The player going out scores for all his melds, plus a bonus of 5 points for going out. The other player or players score for all melds they can form.

For example, in a 2-player game Mike goes out with the following hand: ♣K-♣Q-♣J, ♡A-♠A-◇A, ♡6-♠6-◇6, ♠A-♠2-♠3, ♠4-♠5-♠6. He scores 3 points for the royal assembly, 1 point for the aces, 2 points for the triplet, and 1 point for each of the sequences. This plus the 5 points for going out gives him a total of 13 points. Norman has the following cards: ♡8-♠8-◇8, ♡8-♠8-◇8, ♣J-◇7-♡7, ♡3-♡4-♡5-♡6-♡7, ♠9. He scores 10 points for the double triplet, 4 points for the court meld, and 1 point for the sequence for a total of 15 points.

Winning the Game The scores for a hand are written down. Then the player to the left of the previous dealer deals a new hand. Continue until a total of 50 or over is reached. If two or more players go over 50, the higher total wins. In case of a tie, all players play another hand.

The Game for 4 Players The rules are the same except that all 61 cards are dealt out and there is no drawing deck. Each discard must be picked up by the player to the left unless one of the following happens:

1. One of the other two players bumps the discard.
2. If the player has the identical card, either in his hand or on the table from a previous bump, he may, if desired, show this card and pass the discard to the next player.

KOWAH from Java.

Number of players 2 to 4.

Difficulty level Easy—not many choices to make. But remembering the cards that have been played helps.

Object To get a certain card to complete your hand.

The Deck From each of four regular decks, take the same 30 cards as in Sampen, making a deck of 120 cards. Pictures and aces are all considered 1's.

The Deal Eight cards are dealt to each player, two at a time. The rest of the cards are placed face down in the center of the table as a drawing deck.

The Play The player to the dealer's left takes the top card from the drawing deck and discards a card face up. Each player, in turn, takes the top card from either the drawing deck or the discard pile and then discards.

Checki Players attempt to arrange their cards into 2 sets of 3 cards of equal rank, regardless of suit, and 2 identical cards. When this is accomplished, the player announces "checki" and places the 2 identical cards face down on the table before him. *For example, checki could be announced with the following hand:* ♡3-♡3-♡3, ♡5-◇5-♠5, ♣Q-♣Q.

Checki can also be announced with a hand consisting of a set of 3 cards of the same rank and 5 cards of another rank divided into 2 pairs of identical cards and a single card. The 5 cards are placed face down on the table. *For example, checki could be announced with* ◇8-◇8-♠8, ♡2-♡2-◇2-◇2-♠2.

As soon as the first player announces checki, the play changes. A checki player can claim a discard that adds a third identical card to a pair he has on the table regardless of who discards it. Also, as each card is taken from the drawing deck it is exposed so that a checki player can claim it. A checki player on his turn simply draws a card and discards it, unless of course it would add a third identical card to his pair.

Winning A player wins by adding a third identical card to a pair on the table. If the card was drawn by an opponent, it is a single game. If the card was discarded from an opponent's hand, it is a double game. If the card was drawn by the player himself, it is a triple game.

The winner of a game deals for the next game. If no player wins by the time the drawing deck runs out, the game is ended without a winner, and the same dealer deals again.

TOTIT   from Java.

Number of players   2 to 6.

Difficulty level   Easy—just keep your eyes open.

Object   To score points by getting pairs of identical cards.

The Deck   Use the same deck as for Sampen. Pictures and aces are all considered 1's.

The Deal   When 2 play, deal 11 cards to each. When 3 to 6 play, deal 7 cards to each. In all cases, 18 cards are dealt face up on the table, placed so that all can be seen. The best way is to deal a round of 1 card to each player followed by 3 cards to the table, until the 18 table cards are placed. If fewer than 6 are playing, some cards will remain. These are placed aside until the next deal.

The Play   Starting with the player to the dealer's left, each player in turn either uses a card from his hand to capture a card from the table or places a card face up on the table. On each player's first turn a card can only be captured from the table with an identical card. After this any card of the same rank can be used. *For example the ♠A is on the table. On a player's first turn only the other ♠A could be used to capture it. Later it could be captured by any A or any picture.*

If two identical cards are on the table, as well as one or more of the same rank, the identical cards cannot be captured before the others of that rank. As a player makes captures, the cards are placed face down in a pile before the player. Continue until all the cards have been played. If fewer than 6 are playing, there will probably be uncaptured cards remaining on the table. These are discarded.

Scoring and Winning   The players go through their card piles looking for identical pairs. Each identical pair scores 1 point. The scores are recorded and a new hand is dealt by the player to

11

the left of the previous dealer. Continue until each player has dealt once. The player with the highest score is the winner. In case of a tie, those tying play another hand, cutting cards to see who deals.

Variations For a more challenging game try either or both of the following:

1. An identical pair of 9's scores 3 points. An identical pair of 1's scores 2 points. All other identical pairs score 1 point.

2. As players get cards, they are placed face up in front of the player and spread so that all can be seen.

KABU from Japan, but I have made some changes to make it into a home game rather than a pure gambling game.

Number of players 2 to 6.

Difficulty level Easy, as long as you can add a few numbers.

Object To get your cards to add up to 9 or as close below it as possible.

The Deck Japanese cards are really beautiful, with pictures of flowers and trees representing the twelve months of the year. But for playing this game a regular deck works better. Just eliminate all the pictures, leaving 40 cards.

Chips For keeping score you'll need some chips, the amount varying with the number of players. The table below gives the amounts, but don't worry if you change them a little.

Number of Players	White (1 point)	Red (5 points)	Blue (10 points)
2	10	2	2
3	10	3	3
4	10	4	4
5	10	5	5
6	10	6	6

The Deal It doesn't matter who deals, so usually one player continues until he gets tired, then another player takes over. Although only a few cards may be used in a deal, all the cards are shuffled and cut before each deal. Two cards are dealt to each player.

The Play Each player looks at his cards but leaves them face down on the table. Depending on the total of the first two cards, a player may ask for a third card, also face down. After adding this, a player may get a final fourth card, again face down.

Players try to get as close to a total of 9 as possible. If they go above 9 they are not eliminated; instead only the final digit counts. *For example, a player's first two cards are an 8 and a 5, totaling 13 but counting as 3. The player takes a third card which is a 7. His count is now 0, the worst possible. The fourth card is an 8, making the count an 8, close to the desired 9. If the fourth card had been a 10, the count would have remained 0.*

The Payoff After the players have taken the cards they wish, the cards are exposed and the counts announced. Each player collects chips from all players with a lower count and pays to all players with a higher count. The amount of payment is the difference between the two counts. *For example, four players end up with the following counts: Robin, 6; Steve, 3; Tom, 6; Ursula, 8. Steve pays 5 to Ursula and 3 each to Robin and Tom. Robin and Tom each pay 2 to Ursula.*

Ending the Game If at a payoff a player finds that he does not have enough chips to pay all those who are owed, the player does not pay out *any* chips. The game ends at this point and the player with the most points in chips is the winner.

Players may instead pick a time for the game to end. When this time is reached, the player with the most points wins.

Variation Before cards are dealt to the players, 6 cards are placed face up in the center of the table. This gives the players a clue as to which cards are more likely to come to them.

AS NAS from Persia, which is now called Iran. Many authorities believe that Poker developed from this game.

Number of players 2 to 8.

Difficulty level Medium—the actual rules are simple, but knowing when to bet and when to drop out can take a lot of thought.

Object To win chips by betting wisely.

The Deck When 2, 3, or 4 play, use only the A's, K's, Q's, J's, and 10's from a regular deck. When more play, add one set of A,

K, Q, J, and 10 for each additional player—the suit making no difference.

Chips The available chips are divided equally among the players. Each player should have at least 50 points in chips. If, however, a player runs out of chips during the game, he simply borrows from a player who has more. At the end of the game, any loans not paid back are considered when counting how many points each player has.

The Ante Each player places 1 point (or more if the players agree) into a pool in the center of the table; this is called anteing.

The Deal Five cards are dealt to each player, one at a time.

Rank of Hands In determining which player will win the pool, the hands rank as follows, starting with the strongest:

> *5 of a kind*—5 cards of the same rank (only possible when 5 or more are playing)
>
> *4 of a kind* and 1 unmatched card
>
> *Full house*—3 cards of one rank and 2 cards of another rank
>
> *3 of a kind* and 2 unmatched cards
>
> *2 pair*—2 cards of one rank, 2 cards of another rank, and 1 unmatched card
>
> *1 pair* and 3 unmatched cards.

In case of a tie, the higher rank wins, with A the highest. (Some examples: **Q-Q-Q**-10-10 would beat **J-J-J**-A-A; K-K-**K-A**-10 would beat K-K-**K-Q**-J; **A-A**-10-10-J would beat **K-K**-Q-Q-J; A-A-10-10-**Q** would beat A-A-10-10-**J**.) If the tying hands are exactly the same, the pool is split between them.

Betting Before starting the game, the players should agree on a betting limit. Beginners can start with a limit of 2 points, possibly changing it later.

The player to the dealer's left starts by either passing or by betting 1 or 2 points, placing them in the pool. If the first player passes, the next player may pass or bet 1 or 2 points. If the first player bets, the next player may "drop" (withdrawing from the play of the hand) or may "stay in" (putting in the points previously bet) or may "raise" (putting in the points previously bet plus 1 or 2 more). This continues until, after a bet or a raise, all the other players either drop or stay in.

This sounds a little complicated, but an example should help to clear it up: Alice (to the dealer's left) starts by passing. Bob then bets 2, putting them in the pool. Carol stays in by putting 2 in the pool. Don puts in 2 points and then raises with 1 more point. Earl (the dealer) covers the 3 points from the previous bet and then raises another 2 points. Alice pays 5 points to stay in. Bob pays 3 points (to cover Don's and Earl's raises) and then raises 1 point himself. Carol would have to pay 4 points to stay in and instead drops. Don stays in with 3 points (to cover Earl's and Bob's raises). Earl stays in with 1 point (to cover Bob's raise). Alice also stays in with 1 point.

No player has raised since Bob's last raise, so the betting is ended. Notice that Alice, Bob, Don, and Earl have each put 6 points into the pool during the betting.

The Showdown After the betting, all players who did not drop show their hands. The player with the best hand takes all the chips in the pool.

If all the players drop except one, that player wins the pool without showing his hand.

Ending the Game The players usually pick a time at which the play will end. The player with the most points in chips at that time is the winner.

3
Games from Europe

LA MALILLA (la mahl ēl' yah) ("the malicious one") from Spain.

Number of players 2 to 4.

Difficulty level Fairly hard—keeping track of two different special suits and then counting the point cards takes some skill.

Object To win tricks and to win counting cards in these tricks.

The Game for 4 as Partners This will be described first. The differences when 4 play individually, when 3 play, and when 2 play will be given later.

The Deck Eliminate the 10's from a regular deck, leaving 48 cards. The cards rank in a different order from the usual, with the 9 (called the "malilla") the highest. This is followed by the A, K, Q, J, 8, 7, down to 2. Some of the cards have a point value as follows:

| | POINTS | |
	FAVORITO SUIT	OTHER SUITS
9	10	5
A	8	4
K	6	3
Q	4	2
J	2	1

Choosing Partners The players all cut cards. The two players with the highest cards are partners against the other two. Partners are seated across from each other. The player who cut the highest card deals for the first hand. (If desired, the players

16

may choose partners themselves, just cutting to see who deals.)

The Deal Twelve cards are dealt to each player, either three or four at a time. Before picking up his cards, the dealer turns one face up and shows it to all the players. The suit of this card sets the trump for the deal. After looking at his cards, the dealer chooses any suit—including the trump suit if he wishes—as the "favorito" (favorite). The point value of cards in this suit count double.

The Play The player to the dealer's left starts by leading any card. The other three players in turn play a card. If a player has a card of the suit led, he must follow suit; if not the player may either throw a trump or throw off a card of another suit.

The highest card of the suit led wins the trick unless a trump or trumps are played, in which case the highest trump wins. The winner of one trick leads next.

Scoring Each trick taken counts 1 point, except the first and last tricks which count 2 points each—making a total count of 14 for tricks. The counting cards that each team has taken are totaled, remembering that the favorito suit counts double—making a total of 75 points for counting cards. The points for tricks and for counting cards combine to a grand total of 89.

The team with the higher total scores for each point above the average count of 44 (89 divided by 2). The other team scores nothing. *For example, one team counts 61 points and the other team counts 28 points. The first team scores 61 − 44 = 17; the other scores 0.* If one team wins all the tricks it scores 89 rather than 45.

Ending the Game The score for a hand is recorded, and then the player to the previous dealer's left deals the next hand. When four hands have been played, the team with the higher total score wins. In case of a tie, two more hands are played.

The Game for 4, Each Playing Individually The rules are the same, except for the scoring. Each player with a count over 22 (89 divided by 4) scores for each point over 22. One, two, or three players may score on a hand. *For example, Doris counts 24 points, Esther counts 27 points, Frank counts 3 points, and Grant counts 35 points. Doris scores 2, Esther scores 5, Frank scores 0, and Grant scores 13.* If one player wins all the tricks he scores 89.

If after four hands have been played there is a tie for highest score, those players tying share the victory.

The Game for 3 The rules are the same except for the deck used and the scoring.

From a regular deck eliminate the 2's, 3's, 4's, as well as the 10's, leaving 36 cards.

Each player with a count over 29 (89 divided by 3) scores for each point over 29. If one player wins all the tricks, he scores 89.

If after three hands have been played there is a tie for highest score, those players tying share the victory.

The Game for 2 The rules are the same, except for the following changes:

The deck is made up by eliminating the 10's, A's, 3's, and 2's from a regular deck, leaving 36 cards. With the A's gone, the counting cards total 55 points.

The dealer deals 12 cards to each player and the other 12 are placed face down in the center of the table as a drawing deck. After each trick, the winner draws the top card and the loser takes the next until the drawing deck is gone.

Before the drawing deck is exhausted, a player does not have to follow suit if he doesn't wish to, instead he is allowed to trump or throw off another suit. Once the drawing deck is gone, a player must follow suit if able.

The player with the higher total scores for each point over 37 (75—55 for counting cards plus 20 for tricks—divided by 2). If one player wins all the tricks he scores 75.

The game consists of four hands, each player dealing twice. If a tie results, two more hands are played.

LA MOSCA (la mōs' kah) (means either "fly" or "impertinent intruder" or "money in hand" or "trouble" —after playing you can choose) from Spain.

Number of players 3 to 6.

Difficulty level Medium.

Object To earn shares of a pool by winning tricks.

The Deck The cards used depend on the number of players, as shown in the table below. The ranking of the cards is also indicated, with K the highest.

NUMBER OF PLAYERS	CARDS USED	TOTAL
6	KQJA98765432	48
5	KQJA9876543	44
4	KQJA98765	36
3	KQJA9876	32

Chips Each player gets an equal point value of chips, with from 70 to 100 being a suitable amount.

The Deal The dealer starts by placing 5 points into a pool. Then he deals 5 cards to each player, 1 at a time. The next card is turned face up and left where all players can see it. That suit is trump for the deal.

Dropping or Staying Starting with the player to the dealer's left, each player in turn decides whether he will "drop" (placing his hand face down on the table before him and withdrawing from the play) or "stay." A player who stays may, but does not have to, discard 1, 2, or 3 cards and get replacements from the dealer. If a player discards, he may not decide to drop after seeing the replacements. If all the players before the dealer drop, the dealer takes the pool without further play.

Flush A player with a flush (all 5 cards of the same suit), either dealt or after getting replacements, waits until all players have decided whether to drop or stay. He then shows the flush, takes the pool, and receives 5 points from each player who stayed.

If more than one player has a flush, a trump flush is highest. Otherwise, the 5 cards of each flush are totaled (with pictures and A's counting 10) and the high total wins.

The Play If no flush is shown and two or more players have stayed, the cards are then played out. The remaining player closest to the left of the dealer starts by leading a card. The other players in turn must follow suit if able and must "head" the trick if possible. This means that if a player has a card of the suit led that is higher than any played on the trick so far, the player must play it. Also, a player out of the suit must play a trump, unless a higher trump than any he holds has already been played for that trick. In that case any suit may be thrown. The winner of the trick leads next.

Collecting and Paying For each trick he wins, a player takes one fifth of the points from the pool. Any player who stayed and wins no tricks must place 5 points into the pool for the next hand.

Ending the Game After each hand the player to the left of the previous dealer places 5 points into the pool, deals a new hand, turns a trump, etc.

The players can agree to end the game whenever all players have dealt an equal number of hands. If any points are in the pool from the hand just completed, the cards are cut to determine the dealer for a final hand. He does not pay to the pool, no cards may be exchanged, and all players stay in. The winners of tricks collect in the usual manner. Those winning no tricks do not have to pay.

BRISCOLA (brēs kō′ lah) from Italy.

Number of players 2 to 4.

Difficulty level Easy—you only have to handle 3 cards at a time.

Object To win counting cards.

The Deck Remove the 10's, 9's, and 8's from a regular deck, leaving 40 cards. In each suit the cards rank as shown below, with A the highest.

A ◊	3 ◊	K ◊	Q ◊	J ◊	7 ◊	6 ◊	5 ◊	4 ◊	2 ◊

The point values of the cards are as follows: A, 11 points; 3, 10 points; K, 4 points; Q, 3 points; J, 2 points; the others have no point value.

The Game for 4 The directions given are for 4 players; the small differences when 3 or 2 play will be given later.

Choosing Partners Players either agree on partnerships or cut cards, the two high against the two low. Partners are seated across from each other.

The Deal Three cards are dealt to each player, one at a time. The next card is turned face up and this suit is trump for the hand. The remainder of the deck is placed face down, partially covering the trump card.

The Play The player next to the dealer leads any one of his 3 cards. Each player in turn throws a card. A player is not required to follow suit and may trump or throw another suit. The highest card of the suit led wins the trick unless trump is played, in which case the highest trump wins.

The winner of the trick takes the top card from the drawing deck and each player in turn similarly draws to return his hand to 3 cards. The winner of a trick leads next.

When the drawing deck is exhausted, the last player takes the card turned for trump. Each player then passes his 3 cards to his partner, who looks at them and passes them back. Then the final 3 tricks are played.

Scoring and Winning Each team totals the point values (as noted under The Deck) for all the counting cards they have captured and the scores are recorded. A second hand is dealt by the player next to the previous dealer and then played and scored. The team with the higher total score for the two hands is the winner. In case of a tie, another hand is played.

Exchanging Information Partners are free to talk to each other about the cards they hold. The opponents, of course, can listen. And you may bluff or exaggerate if you think you will fool the opponents more than you'll fool your partner.

The Game for 3 A 2 of any suit is removed, reducing the deck to 39 cards. The play is the same except, of course, that there are no partners. Three hands are played, each player dealing once. Highest total score wins. In case of a tie, another hand is played by all 3.

The Game for 2 The 40-card deck is used. All rules are the same as for 4 except, of course, that there are no partners.

SCOPA (skō′ pah) from Italy.

Number of players 2, 4, or 6.

Difficulty level Easy, as long as you can add up to 10 and at least one player can count higher.

Object To use cards from your hand to capture cards from the table.

The Deck In Italy the deck is the same as that used for Briscola. But Scopa is easier to follow if you eliminate the K's, Q's, and J's from a regular deck, leaving 40 cards. A's are considered 1's.

Partnerships When 4 play they are divided into two teams, either by agreement or by cutting cards, the two high against the two low. When 6 play, they are similarly divided into two teams of 3 players. The players are seated so that they alternate—first a player of one team plays, then a player of the other team.

The Deal Three cards are dealt to each player, and 4 cards are dealt face up in the center of the table. The best way is to deal a round of cards to the players, followed by 2 to the table, another round to the players, another 2 to the table, and a final round to the players.

After the hands have been played, each player is dealt another hand of 3 cards, but no more are dealt to the table. This is repeated until all the cards have been dealt.

The Play Starting with the player next to the dealer, each player in turn plays one card. If there is no card on the table of the same rank, or if no two or more cards on the table add up to that rank, the card is placed face up on the table. *For example, the cards on the table are 7-3-A-9. A player plays a 5, placing it on the table.*

If there is a card of the same rank on the table, the player takes it and places the two cards face down before him. If two or more cards of that rank are on the table, only one can be taken.

If two or more cards on the table add up to the rank of the card played, the player takes them. However, if there is also a card of the same rank on the table, the player must take that instead. *For example, the cards on the table are 7-3-A-9-5. A player playing a 9 must take the 9 rather than the 3, A, and 5. A player playing an 8 may take the 7 and A or the 3 and 5, but not both.*

22

Scoops   If a player taking one or more cards from the table completely clears the table, it is a "scoop." One card is turned face up next to the player's pile of cards to record the scoop.

Remaining Cards   If after all the cards in the final deal have been played there are cards remaining on the table, these go to the last player who took cards. This is not considered a scoop.

Scoring   Each player or team checks for the following scores.

	POINTS
Most cards	1
Most diamonds	1
The ◇7	1
Each scoop	1
Settanta (see below)	1

Settanta   To figure the winner of this point, the cards are given values as follows:

CARD	VALUE	CARD	VALUE
7	21	3	13
6	18	2	12
A	16	10	10
5	15	9	10
4	14	8	10

So to figure Settanta, each player or team takes the highest valued card they have of each of the 4 suits and totals the values of the 4 cards. *For example, a team with* ♠7, 21 points; ♡9, 10 points; ◇7, 21 points; and ♣6, 18 points would have a count of 70 toward settanta. High total wins the point.

Winning   After the scores are recorded, the player next to the previous dealer deals a new hand of cards to the players and the table.

Eleven points are game. Any player who believes that, through scoops and/or the ◇7, he or his team has reached 11 points can stop the play. If correct, that player or team wins— even if the other side has more points. If wrong, the other side wins.

If after the scores are recorded each side has reached 11 points, the higher score wins. In case of a tie, a new hand is started. The first side to score a scoop or take the ◇7 wins.

PIQUET (pē kā) from France.

Number of players 2.

Difficulty level Quite hard, but this is one of the most interesting games for 2 and worth the effort.

Object To score points in several different ways.

The Deck Use the A's, K's, Q's, J's, 10's, 9's, 8's, and 7's from a regular deck for a total of 32 cards. The cards rank as shown, with A high.

The Deal Twelve cards are dealt to each player, two at a time. The remaining eight cards are placed face down between the players.

Discarding The nondealer starts by discarding from 1 to 5 cards (putting them face down to one side) and replacing them from the top of the pile. If fewer than 5 are exchanged, nondealer still looks at those remaining from the 5, replacing them on top of the pile without changing the order. *For example, the non-dealer discards 2 cards and replaces them from the pile. He then picks up 3 cards, looks at them, and returns them to the pile in the same order.*

The dealer may then discard and replace up to all those remaining in the pile, or he may keep his hand. If some cards are not taken, the dealer has the choice of placing them aside face down or face up for both players to see.

A player may look at his discards at any time, but, of course, they may not be put back into play.

Carte Blanche (cahrt blahnsh) If nondealer is dealt 12 cards with no pictures (K's, Q's, or J's), he declares "carte blanche" (which means white card in French), shows the hand, and scores 10 points. (These can be written down, but generally each player keeps track of his score for a hand, announcing the total as each new score is made.) After scoring for carte blanche, the non-dealer discards in the usual manner.

If dealer has carte blanche, he waits until after nondealer has discarded before declaring it. He may then discard in the usual manner.

Declarations After each player has had an opportunity to discard and then restore his hand to 12 cards, there are three categories of declarations that can win points for one player or the other. They are handled in the following order: point, sequence, trio-quartet.

Point Each player looks for his best suit—the one with the most cards, or if two of equal length, the one with the higher point count. In counting a suit, an A counts 11, a picture counts 10, and other cards count their numerical value.

The nondealer announces the length of his best suit. If dealer does not have a suit as long, he says "it's good" and nondealer scores for point. If dealer has a longer suit, he says "it's not good," announces the length of his suit, and scores for point. With the same length, dealer says "equal." Nondealer then announces his suit's count. Dealer again answers either "it's good" or "it's not good" and gives his better count, or "equal." With equal, neither player scores for point.

The winner of point scores 1 point for each card in his longest suit. *For example, Tom's longest suit contains ♠A-♠K-♠Q-♠ J-♠9. As nondealer he announces "five." Ursula, the dealer, holds ◇Q-◇J-◇10-◇9-◇8 and says "equal." Tom then announces "50" as his count. Ursula, with 47, says "it's good," and Tom scores 5 points for point.*

Sequence A sequence is 3 or more cards of the same suit in numerical order. If nondealer has one or more sequences, he announces the length of the longest. Dealer answers "it's good" and nondealer wins for sequence; or "it's not good" and dealer gives his length and wins for sequence; or "equal." After an equal, nondealer announces the highest card in his sequence and dealer answers "it's good" or "it's not good," giving the higher card, or "equal" —in which case neither player scores for sequence.

Sequences score as follows:

Number of Cards	Points
3	3
4	4
5	15
6	16
7	17
8	18

Only the player with the best sequence can score, and also can score for any other sequences held by simply announcing the length of additional sequences.

Continuing the above example, Tom announces a sequence of four. Ursula says "it's not good—five." She also holds ♣Q, ♣J, ♣10 and announces an additional sequence of three. She scores 15 points for the five-diamond sequence and 3 points for the clubs.

Trio-Quartet Three cards of the same rank are a trio; 4 cards of the same rank are a quartet. However, only 10's or better are counted (9's, 8's, or 7's not qualifying as trios or quartets). In determining who scores, a quartet beats a trio and the higher rank wins between quartets or trios.

Since it is easy for a player to figure out what the rank is if the opponent announces a trio or quartet, the declaration is handled in a simpler manner. The nondealer announces his best quartet or trio. Dealer answers "it's good" or "it's not good" and announces the holding that beats it.

A trio scores 3 points. A quartet scores 14 points. The player winning the opportunity to score for trio-quartet can score for all others held. *For example, Tom holds ♠K-♣K-◇K and announces "trio of kings." Ursula holds all four 10's and answers "it's not good—quartet of tens." She also holds ♡Q-◇Q-♣Q. She scores 14 points for the quartet and 3 points for the trio.*

The Play After the declarations are finished, the nondealer leads any card. Suit must be followed if possible. The higher card of the suit led wins the trick, and the winner of one trick leads next.

Counting Each time a player leads a card that is 10 or higher, the player adds 1 point to the points previously earned, announcing the total when leading. Beating the opponent's lead with a card of 10 or higher also scores 1 point.

Following the game between Tom and Ursula, Tom scored 5 for point. Ursula scored 18 points for sequence and 17 points for trio-quartet, making a total of 35. Tom leads the ♣K and announces a score of 6. If Ursula puts on the ♣Q her score remains 35. If she takes the trick with the ♣A, she announces a score of 36.

Note: Many players simplify the scoring by counting 1 point for every lead (even if lower than 10) and 1 point for every time the opponent's lead is taken. Players should agree on which scoring they will use before beginning to play.

Repic If a player (through any combination of points scored from carte blanche, point, sequence, or trio-quartet) reaches a score of 30 or more points before the opponent scores any points, the player wins a bonus of 60 points for repic. *For example, a player scores 6 for point, 15 for sequence, and 14 for quartet, while the opponent scores nothing. The player's score of 35 jumps to 95 for repic.*

Pic If a player (through carte blanche, point, sequence, or trio-quartet plus 1 or more points made during the play for tricks) reaches a score of 30 or more points before the opponent scores any points, the player wins a bonus of 30 points for pic. *For example, a player scores 5 for point, 18 for two sequences, and 6 for two trios, reaching a total of 29 while the opponent remains at 0. If this player is the nondealer, his 1 point for leading adds up to 30 and the score then jumps to 60 with the 30-point bonus for pic. If the player with 29 points is the dealer, the opponent prevents the pic because he gets a point for leading.*

Scoring for Tricks The winner of the last trick scores 1 extra point. The player winning the most tricks scores 10 points; if the tricks are evenly divided, no one scores. If a player wins all 12 tricks, the score is 40 points. This is in place of the score for last trick and for most tricks.

Winning the Game At the end of a hand the scores made by each player are recorded. Six hands are played with the deal alternating. After the six hands, the player with the higher total score is the winner.

The amount of the victory is figured in the following manner. The winner gets a game bonus of 100 points. If the loser reached at least 100 points, the difference between the two scores is added to the winner's bonus. If the loser did not reach 100 points, the scores made by both players is added to the winner's bonus. This occurs even if the winner also did not reach 100 points.

Let's take a few examples to see how this works. At the end of one game, Tom has 193 points and Ursula has 126. The difference between the two scores (67) is added to the 100-point game bonus, making a total of 167. In the next game Tom scores 83 and Ursula scores 151. Since Tom didn't reach 100, Ursula adds both their scores to her bonus for a grand total of 334. In the third game the scores are 96 for Tom and 54 for Ursula. Tom adds both to his 100-point bonus for a grand total of 250.

ECARTE (ā cahrt ā) from France.
Number of players 2.
Difficulty level Easy, but deciding the right time to start the play calls for considerable thought.
Object To win at least 3 of the 5 tricks.
The Deck Discard the 6's through 2's from a regular deck, leaving 32 cards. The cards rank in the order illustrated, with K high.

K♡	Q♡	J♡	A♡	10♡	9♡	8♡	7♡

Chips Nine chips of any color are used for keeping score. At the start of the game they are piled in the center of the table.
The Deal Five cards are dealt to each player—either three at a time followed by two, or two at a time followed by three. The eleventh card is turned face up, setting trump for the deal. If the turned card is a king, the dealer immediately scores 1 point by taking a chip from the central pile.
Exchanging Cards If the nondealer is satisfied with his original cards, he says "I play," and neither player exchanges any cards.

If the nondealer wants to try for a better hand, he says "I propose." Dealer may accept the proposal or refuse it. If refused, neither player exchanges any cards.

If the proposal is accepted, the nondealer discards from 1 to 5 cards and is dealt the same number from the deck, returning his hand to 5 cards. Dealer then can make a similar exchange, or can stay with the cards dealt to him.

After the first exchange, nondealer can again say "I propose" or "I play," and dealer can again accept or refuse. These exchanges continue until one of the following occurs: 1. The nondealer says "I play" or the dealer refuses a proposal. 2. The deck is exhausted. When the number of cards is limited, nondealer has first choice of those remaining, even if none are left for dealer. The card turned for trump cannot be taken by either player.

The Play   If either player holds the king of the trump suit, he shows it and takes a chip from the central pile.

Nondealer leads any card for the first trick. The second player must follow suit if able and must also win the trick, if possible, by playing a higher card of the suit led or by trumping a lead of a nontrump suit when out of that suit. The winner of one trick leads next.

Scoring   The player who stopped the exchanging of cards (nondealer who said "I play" or dealer who refused a proposal) scores 1 point/chip for winning 3 or 4 tricks. For winning all 5 tricks, he scores 2 points/chips. If this player fails to win at least 3 tricks, the opponent scores 2 points/chips.

If the exchanging of cards stopped because the deck was exhausted, either player scores 1 for winning 3 or 4 tricks and scores 2 for winning all 5.

The players alternate in dealing new hands until one player wins by reaching a score of 5 points/chips. If this occurs through the turning or the holding of a trump king, the game ends without further play.

VINGT-ET-UN   (vant ā oon) from France (better known under its English name **BLACKJACK**).
Number of players   2 to 8.
Difficulty level   Easy to start, but the more you study how to play, the better the odds in favor of your winning.

Object To get as close as possible to a total of 21 without going over.

The Deck Use a full deck of 52 cards plus one joker if available (kept separate).

The value of the cards is as follows:

2 to 10	the numerical value
Any picture	10
A	either 1 or 11

To Start Each player gets an equal point value of chips, the more the better. But if a player runs out of chips during the game, he simply borrows from a player who is ahead. Any unpaid loans are taken into consideration in determining who has the most chips at the end of the game.

Any player shuffles the cards and deals them face up, one at a time. When a player receives a black jack (♣J or ♠J), that player becomes the first dealer for the game.

After the deck is shuffled and cut, the dealer places the joker face up at the bottom of the deck. If there is no joker, the dealer takes the top card from the deck and if it is not an ace places it face up at the bottom of the deck. If it is an ace, it is reshuffled into the deck and another card is turned.

The dealer announces the betting limit—the maximum point value of chips that each player can bet for a deal.

Betting and Dealing Before any cards are dealt, each player decides how many points to bet—up to the limit set by the dealer—that his hand will beat the dealer's. These chips are placed in a separate pile in front of the player.

The dealer deals one card face down to each player, then another card face up to each.

The Play If the dealer's face-up card is either a 10, a picture, or an A, the dealer checks his face-down card. If the two cards add up to 21 (any card of value 10, with an A), it is called a "blackjack" or "natural." The cards are shown and the dealer collects the bets from all players who do not also have a natural. Those who also have a natural take back their bets, neither winning nor losing. All the cards dealt are gathered and placed at the bottom of the deck and a new round of hands is dealt from the top.

If the dealer does not have a natural, each player in turn, starting with the player to the dealer's left, proceeds as follows after looking at his face-down card. 1. If the player has a natural, he shows it and collects from the dealer double the bet (also taking back the original chips of course). The cards are placed at the bottom of the deck. 2. If a player is satisfied with the 2 cards dealt (the total is close enough to 21 to have a chance of winning) the player "stands" by placing his bet chips on top of the cards. 3. The player may ask for an additional card. (The usual way is to say "hit me.") This card is dealt face up. The player can continue asking for new cards until he is satisfied and stands, or until he receives a card that brings his total above 21, which is called a "bust." With a bust the player's bet is lost to the dealer and the cards are placed at the bottom of the deck.

After all the players have either stood or gone bust, the dealer has a similar opportunity to stand or to draw cards until satisfied and then to stand, or until he goes bust.

When the dealer goes bust, he pays the amount of the bets to all players who stood.

When the dealer stands, the dealer and all other players who stood, turn up their face-down card. The dealer wins from all players with a lower total and loses to those with a higher total. If the total is the same, the player simply takes back his bet.

Unless one of the players had a natural (see Change of Dealer later), the dealer places all the cards at the bottom of the deck and then deals a new hand.

Reshuffling   When the joker (or other face-up card) is reached, the dealer takes all of the cards below, shuffles them, has them cut, and places them above the face-up joker or other card to form a deck to continue the play.

Change of Dealer   A player who is dealt a natural takes over as the new dealer at the completion of the hand—unless the dealer also was dealt a natural, in which case he keeps dealing. If two or more players are dealt a natural, the one closest to the dealer becomes the new dealer. When a new dealer takes over, he continues using the same deck without reshuffling and announces the new betting limit.

Ending the Game   The usual way is to set a time at which the game will end. At this time the player with the highest point value of chips is the winner.

Some Optional Rules   Many players choose to use one or more of the following rules. Take your pick.

Splitting Pairs   If a player's first 2 cards are a pair, the player may decide to play them as two separate hands, putting the amount of the original bet on each. The face-down card is exposed. On the player's turn, the dealer gives him one face-down card for each card of the pair. The player then plays the two hands separately in any order. Some players do not allow a pair of aces to be split.

Bonuses   A player (but not the dealer) collects the extra amount shown for one of the following hands:
1. 21 with three 7's—collect three times the bet.
2. 21 with 6,7,8—collect double the bet.
3. Standing with 5 cards totaling 21 or less—collect double the bet; 6 cards totaling 21 or less—four times the bet; 7 cards totaling 21 or less—eight times the bet. These hands collect at once, not depending on what the dealer's hand totals later.

Ties to Dealer   When at the end of a hand the dealer and a player each have the same total, the dealer wins the bet.

Rotating the Deal   Instead of changing dealers when a player is dealt a natural, each player in clockwise order deals one hand.

SKAT   (shkaht) from Germany.
Number of players   3.
Difficulty level   Quite hard, but this is undoubtedly the most fascinating game around for 3 players.
Object   By bidding, to become the one to play against the other two and to win tricks with the necessary total of counting cards; or to stop the player who won the bid.
The Deck   From a regular deck discard the 6's down to the 2's, leaving 32 cards. The four jacks are always part of the trump in the following order: ♣J, ♠J, ♡J, ◇J. After these, the order of the suit chosen as trump follows with A, 10, K, Q, 9, 8, 7— making a total of 11 trumps.

For example, if spades are chosen trump, the trumps would rank as shown.

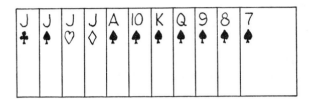

There are 7 cards in each of the other suits, ranking A, 10, K, Q, 9, 8, 7.

Some of the cards have point values as follows:

	POINTS
A	11
10	10
K	4
Q	3
J	2

The Deal The dealer deals 3 cards to each player, then 2 cards to a "skat," another 4 cards to each player, and a final 3 cards to each player. Players end up with hands of 10 cards. The skat is face down on the table.

Bidding The 3 players are given special names, and these are important to know in understanding the bidding. The player to the left of the dealer is called "forehand"; the next player is called "middlehand"; and the dealer is called "endhand."

Players bid for the right to name the type of "game" that will be played (these will be explained a little later). Middlehand starts by passing or by making a bid of a number of points. If middlehand bids and forehand is willing to play at the level bid, forehand says "I stay"; if not, forehand passes. If forehand stays, middlehand can either pass or raise the bid. This continues until one of the two passes. Endhand may now pass or similarly try to bid to a level higher than that at which the surviving player is willing to play.

All bids must be the number of points that are possible from one of the games that can be named (which will be explained shortly).

If both middlehand and endhand pass without making any bids, forehand can name any game without bidding.

The Games The one who names the game is called the "player." There are 15 different games from which the player may choose. In the following two tables, 12 of these games are listed. The number after each game is a base value that will be multiplied (as described later) by at least 2, and possibly by much more, to determine the final value of the game.

Suit Trumps		Jacks Only Trumps	
◇ Tournee	5	Tournee grand	12
♡ Tournee	6	Gucki grand	16
♠ Tournee	7	Solo grand	20
♣ Tournee	8	Open grand	24
◇ Solo	9		
♡ Solo	10		
♠ Solo	11		
♣ Solo	12		

The values for the following 2 games are their final values; they are never multiplied.

Simple null	20
Open null	40

The fifteenth game is called least and its value varies, as described later.

Tournees If the player names tournee, he looks at one card of the skat. If satisfied with that suit as trump, he shows it to the other players, then takes it and the other skat card (without showing it) into his hand. If the first card is a jack, the player has a choice between naming that suit as trump or naming a tournee grand, in which case only the 4 jacks are trump.

If the player is not satisfied with the first card, it is picked up without being exposed and the second card is turned face up. This suit is automatically trump unless the card is a jack, in which case the player may choose a tournee grand instead. Using the second card is called "second turn," and if the player loses, he suffers a double penalty.

After taking up both cards of the skat, the player chooses any 2 cards from his hand and places them face down next to him.

Solos If the player names solo, he chooses the trump suit. If solo grand is named, only the jacks are trump. The player without looking at it places the skat next to him.

A player naming either solo or solo grand may try to increase his score by predicting that he will win all the tricks (announcing "schwarz") or that he will make more than 90 points (announcing "schneider"). If not successful in fulfilling the prediction, the player loses the game.

Gucki Grand Naming this game allows the player to pick up both cards of the skat, without showing them, and then to place 2 cards face down next to him. Only jacks are trump. If the player loses, he suffers a double penalty.

Open Grand The player who names this game places his hand face up on the table before the first card is led. In order to win, the player must take every trick—the same as predicting schwarz. Only jacks are trump and the skat is not picked up.

Nulls This is a completely different type of game. There are no trumps, not even jacks. The cards rank A (high), K, Q, J, 10, 9, 8, 7 and have no point value. The skat is set aside. The player is successful if he doesn't win a single trick.

In a simple null the player keeps his cards in hand. In an open null all of the cards are placed face up on the table before the first card is led.

Least This game can only be named by forehand when neither middlehand nor endhand have made any bid. Jacks are trump. Each player plays alone and tries to take as few points as possible.

The Play Regardless of who named the game, forehand leads to the first trick. Players must follow suit if possible; if not they may throw any suit they wish. The trick is won by the highest card of the suit led unless a trump is played, in which case the highest trump wins. The winner of one trick leads next.

After the last trick, the skat or the two cards placed down are added to the player's tricks. In "least," however, the skat cards go to the one who takes the last trick. In a null, the skat is ignored.

Counting Points When the play is finished in all games

except null and least, the player counts the points among all the cards he holds and, depending on the total, makes one of the following (see also Scoring When Losing):

Game 61 to 90 points

Schneider 91 or more points

Schwarz Every trick (even losing a trick with no points in it stops a schwarz)

Multipliers In previous tables, base values were given for 12 of the possible games. To get the final value for a game, the base value is multiplied by a number determined from the following table:

	MULTIPLIERS
Making game	1
Making schneider	2
Making schwarz	3
Announcing schneider and making it	3
Announcing schneider and making schwarz	4
Announcing schwarz and making it	5

Plus 1 multiplier for each matador, with or without.

Matadors This is a little tricky to understand at first. Matadors are trumps *in an unbroken sequence,* starting with the ♣J. If the player has the ♣J in his original 10 cards or finds it in the skat, he is said to be "with" matadors. If the ♣J is not among any of these cards, he is said to be "without" matadors.

Let's take a few examples. John becomes the player with spades as trump—so look back to the illustration of spades as trump. He holds ♣J, ♠J, ◇J, ♠A, ♠Q... If he finds ♠10 and ♣A in the skat, he is "with 2"—the missing ♡J stopping the sequence. If he finds ♡J and ♣A, he is "with 5"—the missing ♠10 stopping the sequence. If he finds ♡J and ♠10, he is "with 6"—the missing ♠K stopping the sequence.

Suppose Karen becomes the player with a solo grand. She holds ♡J, ◇J, ♣A, ♠A, ♡A, ◇A.... She counts on being "without 2." If she later finds ♠10, ♡8 in the skat, she remains "without 2." If she finds ♠J, ♡8, she is reduced to "without 1." If she finds ♣J, ♠10, she is reduced to "with 1." Finding ♣J, ♠J, she goes up to "with 4."

Scoring The score the player receives for succeeding in a game (except null or least) is figured by multiplying the base value of the game by the number determined from the table of multipliers.

Here are some more examples. John plays a diamond tournee and ends up with 91 points, giving him 2 multipliers for making schneider. He is "with 5" matadors, which brings him to 7 multipliers. A diamond tournee has a base value of 5, so his score is 35.

Karen plays a solo grand and announces schneider. She ends up with 103 points, giving her 3 multipliers for announcing schneider and making it. She is "without 2" matadors, bringing the multipliers to 5. A solo grand has a base value of 20, so her score is 100.

Larry plays an open grand and ends up with all the tricks, giving him 5 multipliers for announcing schwarz and making it. He is "with 3" matadors, bringing the multipliers to 8. An open grand has a base value of 24, so his score is 192.

Scoring When Losing The player can lose in a number of different ways and the scoring is similar to that for winning, as shown in the following:

If the player's point total is from 31 to 60, he has lost a game (1 multiplier).

If the player's point total is less than 31, he has lost a schneider (2 multipliers).

If the player takes no tricks, he has lost a schwarz (3 multipliers).

If the player announces a schneider and fails to make 91 points (3 multipliers).

If the player announces a schwarz and fails to take all of the tricks (5 multipliers).

If the player's point total is enough for the game played but the final value of that game is lower than the amount bid, he also loses. The amount of the loss is the multiple of the game's base value that is equal to or higher than the amount bid. *For example, Karen bids 60, expecting to play a solo grand "without 2" matadors. She gets a point total of 87, but when she looks at the skat she finds the ♣J, which reduces her to "with 1" matador. The final value of the game is now only 40—the solo grand's base* value of 20 times a multiplier of 2. She loses 60, the multiple of 20 that equals her bid. If her bid had been 50, she would still lose 60. *If her point total reached 91, the extra multiplier for schneider would have saved her.*

If the player plays a tournee (second turn) or a gucki grand and loses, the base value for that game is doubled. *For example, Larry picks a spade tournee on the second turn. He gets a point total of only 24—2 multipliers for a lost schneider. He is "with 1" matador, bringing the multipliers to 3. The spade tournee's base value of 11 is doubled to 22. Larry loses 66.*

Scoring a Null This is easy. The player scores 20 for a simple null or 40 for an open null if he does not take a single trick. If he takes a trick, he loses the same amount.

Scoring a Least The one who takes the fewest points scores 10, or 20 for taking no tricks. If all three tie with 40 points, forehand scores the 10. If two players tie for low, the one who did not take the last trick scores the 10; if neither took the last trick, each scores 5. If one player takes all the tricks, he loses 30 and the others score nothing.

Settling Up The scores are recorded on paper, keeping a running total for each player. When a player loses, the amount is deducted from his previous score; it is possible to end up with a minus number (below zero).

The players usually choose a time at which play will end, except that it continues until each player has been the dealer an equal number of times.

At the end of play, each player loses to any player with a higher score and by the difference between their scores. *For example, John ends up with 89, Karen ends up with 145, and Larry ends up with −66. To make the figuring easier, add 66 to each player's score, with the following results: John, 155; Karen, 211; Larry, 0. Larry loses 211 to Karen and 155 to John. John loses 56 to Karen.*

SECHS UND SECHZIG (zex oond zex' tsig) **(SIXTY-SIX)** from Germany.
Number of players 2.
Difficulty level Medium.

Object To be the one to reach a score of 66 or more points by marriages, by taking in counting cards, and by winning the last trick.

The Deck From a regular deck discard the 8's down to the 2's, leaving 24 cards. Cards rank as follows: A (high), 10, K, Q, J, 9. All of the cards except 9's have a point value as shown:

	POINTS
A	11
10	10
K	4
Q	3
J	2

The Deal Six cards are dealt to each player, three at a time. The next card is turned face up and sets the trump for the deal. The rest of the cards are placed face down, partially covering the trump card, to form a drawing deck.

The Play The nondealer leads. While the drawing deck remains, it is not necessary to follow suit, so the second player may throw any card. The trick is won by the higher card of the suit led or by trumping.

The winner of a trick takes the top card from the drawing deck and the loser takes the next .When only one card remains in the drawing deck, the winner takes this and the loser takes the face-up card. The winner of one trick leads next.

Taking the Trump Card After winning a trick and just before leading next, a player with the 9 of trumps may exchange it for the face-up trump card. If a player draws the 9 of trumps as the last card in the deck, he may not make the exchange, since the opponent will have already picked up the trump card.

Marriages A king and a queen of the same suit is called a "marriage." A trump marriage scores 40; a plain marriage scores 20. A player claims a marriage after winning a trick by showing the two cards and then leading one of them. If the nondealer wishes to lead a card from a marriage for the first trick, he shows the marriage and makes the lead. The score, however, is not counted until he wins a trick, and he is not permitted to claim another marriage in the lead after this trick.

Closing the Deck On his turn a player may "close the deck" just before leading. This is indicated by turning the trump card face down. No further cards are taken from the drawing deck and the rules for Play of the Last 6 Cards start with this trick.

Play of the Last 6 Cards After the drawing deck is exhausted or after the deck is closed, a player must follow suit if able; otherwise any card can be played. Marriages may be claimed in the usual manner during this period.

Scoring Points are scored for capturing counting cards, for claiming marriages, and for winning the last trick (10 points). If the deck was closed, the score for last trick is not counted.

Game Points If only one player reaches a score of 66 or more points, he wins game points as follows:

	GAME POINTS
Opponent's score is 33 or more	1
Opponent's score is less than 33 (schneider)	2
Opponent has not won a trick (schwarz)	3

If both players have exactly 65 points or if both players have 66 or more points (even if one has more points than the other), neither wins game points for the deal. But the winner of the next deal will win 1 additional game point.

If a player closed the deck and does not reach a score of at least 66, the opponent wins 2 game points, regardless of his score. If a player closed the deck before the opponent took a trick and fails to reach 66, the opponent wins 3 game points.

If a player is pretty sure he has reached 66 points, the player can stop the play at any time. If correct, the player wins game points as shown in the chart, winning 1 point even if the opponent has a score of 66 or more. If wrong, the opponent wins 2 game points.

Winning The player reaching a total of 7 or more game points is the winner.

BEZIQUE (bā zēk) from Sweden. (Invented by a Swedish schoolmaster, this game received its present name and its greatest popularity in France.)

Number of players 2.

Difficulty level Hard—there are quite a few different things to keep an eye on.

40

Object   To score points by building and declaring melds and by winning counting cards in tricks.

The Deck   From two regular decks remove all the 6's down to the 2's, leaving 64 cards. The cards rank A (high), 10, K, Q, J, 9, 8, 7. The aces and tens are called "brisques" and count 10 points each when won in tricks.

The Deal   Eight cards are dealt to each player—three, two, and three at a time. The seventeenth card is turned face up, setting trump for the deal. The remainder of the cards are placed face down, partially covering the trump card to form a drawing deck.

If the turned trump is a 7, the dealer scores 10 points for it. Each player keeps a running total of the points he receives during a deal, announcing the new total each time a score is made.

The Play   Nondealer leads first. While there are cards remaining in the drawing deck, it is not necessary to follow suit so any card may be thrown. A trick is won by playing a higher card of the suit led or by trumping a plain suit. If two identical cards are played to a trick, the first wins.

The winner of a trick takes the top card from the drawing deck and the opponent takes the next. On the final draw, the second player will take the face-up card. The winner of one trick leads next.

Melds   The table shows the various melds that can be made and the points scored for making them.

	POINTS
Royal marriage (K and Q of trumps)	40
Common marriage (K and Q of another suit)	20
Sequence (A-10-K-Q-J of trumps)	250
Bezique (♠Q and ◇J)	40
Double bezique	500
Any four A's	100
Any four K's	80
Any four Q's	60
Any four J's	40

Each time a player wins a trick, the player is permitted to declare and score one meld. This is done before taking a card from the drawing deck.

41

The player places the cards forming the meld face up on the table before him and adds the score to any scores that may have been previously made that deal. The cards remain on the table but are still a part of the player's hand and are played to tricks in the usual way.

A smaller meld can be scored and then have cards added to it to score as a larger meld. If the larger meld is scored first, the smaller meld may not be scored later. *For example, Sylvia melds the K and Q of trump, scoring 40. With the K and Q still on the table, she later adds the A-10-J and scores 250 for a sequence. If the sequence had been scored first, she could not later score for the royal marriage. As another example, Tom melds ♠Q and ◇J, scoring 40. He later adds another ♠Q and ◇J, scoring 500 for a double bezique. If the double bezique had been scored first, he could not later score for the single.*

A card may not be used twice in the same meld, but may be used in different melds. *For example, Sylvia wins a trick and scores 60 for melding*

In the course of play she throws off the ♣Q and then wins another trick. She cannot add another queen to the three on the table and score queens again. She can, however, add the ♠K and score 20 for a common marriage—spades are not trumps.

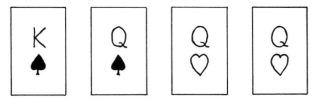

She wins the next trick with a ♡Q and adds the ◇J, scoring 40 for bezique.

She could, after winning another trick, add ♣K-♡K-◇K and score 80 for kings. The ♡K and ♡Q already on the table could then be melded the next time a trick is won.

The 7 of Trumps A player who holds a 7 of trumps may, after winning a trick, score 10 points for it. The player may not make a meld at the same time. If a higher trump card is faced beneath the drawing deck, the player may exchange the 7 for it after taking the score.

Play of the Last 8 Cards After the drawing deck is exhausted, each player picks up any meld cards that may remain on the table. The play now changes. Suit must be followed and the second player must win the trick if possible by playing a higher card of the suit led or by trumping if out of the suit. No melds may be declared during this play, nor may a player score 10 points for a 7 of trumps. The player winning the last trick adds 10 points to his score.

Scoring After play of a hand is completed, each player counts the brisques (A's and 10's) that he captured in tricks. Each one adds 10 points to the player's score.

Game is 1000 points. If neither player reaches 1000, a new hand is played with the deal alternating. If both players have 1000 or more, the higher score wins. If a tie, continue playing until 1500, crediting the winner with a double game. If the scores are again tied, continue until 2000 for a triple game, etc.

Variation If the players agree to play this variation, no card is turned to set the trump. Instead, the first marriage melded sets that suit as trump. There is no score for 7 of trump.

POLISH BEZIQUE from Poland. This is a fast-scoring version of Bezique with much greater opportunity for making melds. All the rules are the same except for the following changes.

Melds Melds are never made from a player's hand; instead they are formed from cards captured in tricks.

Each time a player wins a trick, all cards that could be used in melds are placed face up before the player and remain there until the end of the play. When one or both of the cards in a trick allow one or more melds to be formed, the player declares the meld or melds and records the score.

For example, diamonds are trumps and Tom has already won tricks containing the cards shown

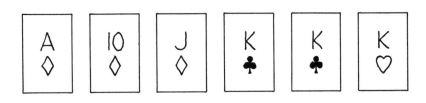

If he wins a trick with ◇K and ◇Q, he scores 250 for sequence (but not the 40 for royal marriage) and 80 for kings. If by the end of the play he can win the other four kings in tricks, he would score another 80 for them.

If a player does not declare a meld at the time he takes the card, or cards, that completes the meld, the player loses the opportunity to declare that meld. In other words, a meld may not be declared that doesn't use a card from the trick the player just won.

The 7 of Trumps A player winning a 7 of trumps in a trick scores 10 points. If a higher trump card is faced beneath the drawing deck, the player exchanges the 7 for it.

Play of the Last 8 Cards Players may continue to declare melds until after the last trick is played. Players, however, do not score 10 points for winning a 7 of trumps during this period.

Scoring Game is 2000 points. In case of a tie above 2000, continue to 2500, etc.

JASS (yahs) from Switzerland.
Number of players 2 to 4.
Difficulty level Medium.
Object To score points by declaring melds and by winning counting cards in tricks.
The Deck From a regular deck remove the 5's, 4's, 3's, and 2's, leaving 36 cards.
The cards rank in the following order:
Trump suit: J (high), 9, A K, Q, 10, 8, 7, 6.
Plain suit: A (high), K, Q, J, 10, 9, 8, 7, 6.
Some of the cards have point values as shown:

	POINTS
J of trumps	20
9 of trumps	14
A	11
10	10
K	4
Q	3
J, plain suit	2

The Game for 2 Players There are quite a few differences in the play, depending on the number playing. The rules for 2 players will be given first, followed by the changes when 3 or 4 play.
The Deal Nine cards are dealt to each player, three at a time. The rest of the cards are placed face down to form a drawing deck. The top card is turned face up and slipped partially under the deck. The suit turned is trump for the deal.
The Play Nondealer leads any card. Until the drawing deck is exhausted, following suit is not required and any card may be thrown. A trick is won by the higher card of the suit led or by the trumping of a plain suit lead.

The winner of a trick takes the top card from the drawing deck and the loser takes the next card. At the final draw, the loser takes the face-up card.

The winner of one trick leads next.
Melds The following table shows the melds that can be made, with the number of points they score:

	POINTS
Four J's	200
Four A's, four K's, or four Q's	100
Five cards of the same suit in sequence	100
Four cards of the same suit in sequence	50
Three cards of the same suit in sequence	20
King and queen of trumps	20

Sequences in all suits (including trumps) follow the usual order for cards, that is A, K, Q, J, 10, 9, 8, 7, 6.

A player who wins a trick may, after taking a card from the drawing deck, declare one meld. The cards are left exposed on the table but can be played in the same way as those still held by the player. The number of points is credited to the player's score.

A player after winning a trick and drawing may add one or more cards to those on the table and score for a new meld. *For example, Alice melds ◇K and ◇Q when diamonds are trump and scores 20. After winning another trick she adds the ◇J and scores 20 for a sequence of 3. She wins a later trick with the ◇K and then adds ◇10-◇9 to the ◇Q-◇J, scoring 50 for a 4-card sequence.*

The 6 of Trumps The player with the 6 of trumps may trade it for the turned trump at any time while there is still a drawing deck. If the winner of a trick draws the 6 of trumps as the last card in the deck, he can no longer make the trade. There is no score for trading the 6 of trumps. It does not stop a player from scoring a meld.

Play of the Last 9 Cards The players pick up any cards that may remain on the table from melds. In this period a player must follow suit and must also win the trick, if possible, by playing a higher card of the suit led or by trumping a plain suit lead when out of the suit.

The jack of trumps (called "jass") has special privileges. It can be used to trump a trick, even if the player has cards of the suit led. Also when trump is led, a player with no other trump than jass does not have to play it if he doesn't wish to.

The player winning the last trick scores 5 points.

Scoring Each player counts the points for cards won in tricks and adds them to any points scored for melds or for winning the last trick.

Game is 1000 points. If neither player reaches 1000, a new hand is played with the other player dealing. If both players reach 1000, higher score wins; with a tie, play another hand.

The Game for 4 Players   All the rules are the same as in the game for 2 except as follows:

The Deal   Nine cards are dealt to each player, three at a time. One of the dealer's cards is turned face up to set the trump suit for the hand. If one of the other players has the 6 of trumps, he trades it for the turned trump and the dealer is stuck with the 6.

The Play   The player to the left of the dealer leads any card. A player must follow suit if able and must, if possible, play a higher card than any already played. If a player is out of a plain suit, he must trump, unless the trick was previously trumped and the player does not have a higher trump. In this case, any card may be thrown.

Jass (jack of trumps) has the same privileges as in Play of the Last 9 Cards when 2 play.

The winner of one trick leads next. The winner of the last trick scores 5 points.

Melds   After the first trick has been played, all players with one or more melds in their hands may show them. The scores for the melds are recorded and the players then return the cards to their hands.

If a player who has melded does not win at least one trick during the play, he loses the score for the melds.

Scoring   Each player counts the points for cards won in tricks and adds them to any points scored for melds or for winning the last trick. If a player fails to make at least 21 points, the player is penalized 100 points and can end up below zero. *For example, Bob makes only 17 points. From previous hands he has a score of 76. Deducting 100 points from this, he ends up with −24.*

Game is 1000 points. New hands are played, with the deal rotating to the left, until at least one player reaches 1000. If 2 or more reach 1000, higher score wins. In case of a tie, all players continue playing, with 1250 the new goal. With another tie, play for 1500, etc.

The Game for 3 Players   All the rules are the same as in the game for 4 except the following:

The Deal Four hands of nine cards each are dealt, three at a time. Each player picks up one hand and the fourth hand remains on the table. One card from this hand is turned face up to set the trump suit.

A player with the six of trumps may exchange it for the face-up trump card. However, if the player intends to take the extra hand, it is better not to make the exchange.

If the dealer wishes, he can discard his entire hand and pick up the extra hand in its place. If the dealer doesn't wish to, the player to the dealer's left and the third player have the same opportunity. After this, whichever cards are on the table are placed aside, out of play.

KLABBERJASS (klah' ber yahs) from the Netherlands.
Number of players 2.
Difficulty level Medium to hard.
Object To score more points than the opponent by naming the proper trump.
The Deck From a regular deck discard the 6's down to the 2's, leaving 32 cards.

The cards rank in the following order: Trump suit: J (high), 9, A, 10, K, Q, 8, 7. Plain suit: A (high), 10, K, Q, J, 9, 8, 7.

Some of the cards have point values:

	POINTS
J of trumps	20
9 of trumps	14
A	11
10	10
K	4
Q	3
J, plain suit	2

The Deal Six cards are dealt to each player, three at a time. The next card is turned face up and placed partly under the deck. This sets the first choice for trumps.
Bidding Nondealer bids first and has three possible bids:
1. *Take*—the suit of the turned card becomes trump and non-dealer is the "trump-maker."
2. *Schmeiss* (pronounced shmice)—a proposal to throw in the

cards and have the same dealer deal again. Dealer may accept or may refuse. If the dealer refuses, the suit of the turned card becomes trump and nondealer is the trump-maker, the same as if he originally said "take".

3. *Pass.*

After a pass by nondealer, dealer may bid:

1. *Take*—the suit of the turned card becomes trump and dealer is the trump-maker.

2. *Schmeiss*—if refused, the suit of the turned card becomes trump and dealer is the trump-maker.

3. *Pass.*

After a pass by dealer, nondealer may bid:

1. *A suit other than that of the turned card as trumps*—nondealer is the trump-maker.

2. *Schmeiss*—if refused, nondealer must name a trump other than that of the turned card and becomes the trump-maker.

3. *Pass.*

After a second pass by nondealer, dealer may bid:

1. *A suit other than that of the turned card as trumps*—dealer is the trump-maker.

2. *Pass*—the cards are thrown in and redealt by the same dealer.

Continued Deal The dealer deals another 3 cards to each player and the remainder of the deck is placed aside, out of play.

If the turned card was chosen for trumps, a player with the 7 of trumps may exchange it for the turned card. There is no score for this exchange.

Sequences Before the play begins, the players may try to score for sequences:

	POINTS
3 cards of the same suit in sequence	20
4 cards of the same suit in sequence	50

Sequences over 4 cards do not score extra points. For the purpose of sequences, all suits follow the order A, K, Q, J, 10, 9, 8, 7 and not the order in which they rank.

Only one player may score. If nondealer has a sequence, he announces "20" or "50," depending on the length. If dealer does not have a sequence of equal length, he answers "good" and nondealer earns the right to score. If dealer has a longer

49

sequence, he answers "no good" and earns the right to score. If dealer has an equal sequence, he says "same."

When dealer says "same," nondealer announces the highest card in his sequence. Dealer again answers "good," "no good," or "same." If two sequences have the same high card, a trump sequence beats a plain suit. If both are plain suits, the nondealer is considered the winner.

If nondealer has no sequences, he announces this and the dealer earns the right to score if he has any sequences.

The player earning the right can score as many sequences as he holds. The sequences are shown to the opponent, the scores are recorded, and the cards are then replaced in the player's hand.

The Play Nondealer leads with any card. Suit must be followed if possible and a trick must be won if possible by playing a higher card of the suit led or by trumping a lead of a plain suit.

The winner of one trick leads next. The winner of the last trick scores 10 points.

Bella If a player holds the king and queen of trump, the player can announce "bella" when the second one is played and score 20 points. A player does not have to announce bella if it is not to his advantage to do so. If the holder of bella was the trump-maker and feels that he will go "bete" (see below for what this means) it is best not to announce it.

Scoring Each player totals his score from sequences, bella, last trick, and counting cards. If the trump-maker has the higher total, both players enter their scores toward game. If the totals are equal, only the opponent of trump-maker enters his score toward game. If the trump-maker has a lower total, he is "bete," and the opponent enters the sum of both players' scores toward game.

Game is 500 points. New hands, with the dealer alternating, are dealt until this is reached. If both players go above 500 points, the higher total wins. In case of a tie above 500, play another hand to break the tie.

SOLO WHIST from Belgium (also called **WHIST DE GAND** or **GHENT WHIST**).
Number of players 4 (or 3).

Difficulty level Hard.

Object By being the high bidder, to name the type of game to be played; and then to win, or lose, the required number of tricks.

Chips Although pencil and paper may be used, it is easier to use chips for keeping score. Each player starts with an equal point value. If a player runs out of chips, he simply borrows from a player who is ahead. Unpaid debts are taken into consideration when checking who has the most points at the end of the game.

The Game for 4 This is the usual number of players. An adaptation for 3 players is given later.

The Deck A regular 52-card deck, ranking in the regular order.

The Deal Thirteen cards are dealt to each player, three at a time, and then finally a round of one card to each. The dealer's last card is turned face up to set the favored trump suit.

Bidding Players bid for the right to name the type of game to be played. The 7 possible bids are listed below, with number 1 the lowest and number 7 the highest.

1. *Proposal*—one player bids this. If one of the other three players "accepts" and there are no higher bids, the two players become partners for this hand. They do not change seats even if they are seated next to each other. The suit of the turned card is trumps and the partners are successful if together they win 8 tricks.

2. *Solo*—a bid to win 5 tricks playing alone against the other three players. The suit of the turned card is trumps.

3. *Misere*—a bid to lose every trick. There is no trump.

4. *Abundance*—a bid to win 9 tricks playing alone. The player will name a suit other than that of the turned card as trumps.

5. *Abundance in trumps*—a bid to win 9 tricks playing alone and with the turned suit as trumps.

6. *Open misere*—a bid to lose every trick, playing with the hand exposed. The bidder's hand is placed face up on the table after the first trick has been played, but before the winner of the first trick leads to the second. There is no trump.

7. *Slam*—a bid to win every trick, playing alone and with no trump.

51

The player to the left of the dealer starts by making a bid or by passing. Each player in turn may accept a proposal if one was offered, may make a bid higher than any previously made, or may pass. Once a player passes, he may not enter the bidding again, except that the player to the dealer's left may accept a proposal after having passed at the start.

The player to the dealer's left has another privilege. If he starts with a proposal and the other three players pass, the player may make another bid (which, since the others have passed, is the winning bid) or may also pass.

If all four players pass, or if a proposal is followed by three passes, the hands are thrown in and the next player to the left deals.

The Play   If the winning bid was a slam, the bidder leads to the first trick, regardless of his position in respect to the dealer. In all other cases the player to the left of the dealer makes the first lead.

A player must follow suit if able. If not, he may throw any suit, including trump. The highest card of the suit led wins the trick unless it is trumped, in which case the highest trump wins. The winner of one trick leads next.

Once a player or a partnership has won the required number of tricks, play of the hand can stop. It can also stop when it becomes impossible for the bid to be successful.

Scoring   The following table shows the payments for each of the bids. If the bidder is successful, he collects that many points from each opponent; if unsuccessful, he pays that amount to each opponent. With proposal and acceptance each of the partners collects from or pays to each of the opponents (so that all players either win or lose 4 points).

BID	POINTS
Proposal and acceptance	2
Solo	2
Misere	3
Abundance	4
Abundance in trumps	4
Open misere	6
Slam	8

Extra Points   If the players agree to this variation, the hands are played to the end and extra points are won or lost as follows: an extra point is collected for each trick a player or a partnership takes that is over the number necessary to succeed in the bid; if the bid is missed by more than one trick, an extra point is paid for each such trick.

For example, Sylvia plays an abundance. If she wins 9 tricks, she collects 4 points from each of the other three players; if she wins 10 tricks, she collects 5 points; if she wins 11 tricks, she collects 6 points; etc. If she wins 8 tricks, she pays 4 points to each of the other three players; if she wins 7 tricks, she pays 5 points; etc.

Extra points do not apply when either a misere, an open misere, or a slam is played. Play is stopped as soon as the bidder wins a trick in one of the miseres or loses a trick in a slam.

Winning   Usually a time is set for winding up the game. When this time is reached, play continues until all players have had an equal number of chances to deal. The player with the most points in chips is the winner.

Variation   Some players, instead of throwing in the cards when all 4 players pass or when a proposal is followed by 3 passes, play the hand with no trump. The player who takes the last trick pays 2 points in chips to each of the other 3 players.

The Game for 3   The rules are the same as in the game for 4, except for the following changes.

The Deck   From a regular deck eliminate the 4's, 3's, and 2's, leaving 40 cards.

The Deal   Thirteen cards are dealt to each player, three at a time and then finally a round of one card to each. The fortieth card is turned face up to set the favored trump suit. This card belongs to no player.

Bidding   Proposal and acceptance are not used. All other bids are the same as in the game for 4.

VINT   from Russia.
Number of players   4.
Difficulty level   Easy rules, but the scoring can become quite complicated.

Object To bid for the right to name the trump and then to make at least as many tricks as were bid.

The Deck A regular 52-card deck, ranking in the regular order.

To Start The 4 players are divided into 2 teams, either by choice or by each player cutting a card, the 2 high cards forming 1 team and the 2 low cards the other. Partners are seated across from each other.

WE	THEY

You'll need a score sheet that looks like the one shown, but leave plenty of room for a lot of scoring.

The Deal Thirteen cards are dealt to each player, one at a time.

Bidding Bids are made in numbers from 1 to 7. A bid indicates the number of tricks over 6 that the team making the bid expects to capture. (Thus to be successful in a bid of 1, a team would have to take 7 tricks. To be successful in a bid of 2, a team would have to take 8 tricks. To be successful in a bid of 7, a team would have to take all 13 tricks.)

In making a bid, a player also names a suit as trump or no-trumps. These rank in the following order, with no-trumps the highest: no-trumps, hearts, diamonds, clubs, spades.

Starting with the dealer, each player in turn must bid or pass. Once a bid is made, a following bid must be higher—in rank, in number of tricks, or both. *For example, a bid of 1—in diamonds can be overbid by 1—in hearts, or 1—in no-trumps, or 2—in spades, or 2—in clubs, or 2—in diamonds, or 2—in hearts, etc.*

The bidding continues until a bid by one player is followed by the other three players passing. Until this happens a player on his turn can always bid—even if the player previously passed or if the player is only raising a bid made by his partner. (A team's score is based on how many tricks they bid, so it is to their

54

advantage to bid as high as they safely can, even if the other team is not bidding against them. Also, one member of a team can be telling his partner that it would be better to play with a different suit as trump or with no-trumps.)

If all 4 players pass at the start, the cards are thrown in and a new hand is dealt by the next dealer.

The Play The player to the left of the player who made the highest bid starts by leading any card. Suit must be followed if possible. If a player has no cards of the suit led, he may trump (except of course at no-trumps) or throw off another suit. The highest card of the suit led wins the trick, unless it is trumped, in which case the highest trump wins. The winner of one trick leads next.

Scoring Toward Game Each team scores for every trick they take. (Even if the team making the highest bid is not successful in taking the number of tricks bid, they still score for the tricks they do take. They are given a different penalty which will be explained later.)

The scoring value of each trick depends on the number of tricks in the final bid. If the bid was 1, each trick is worth 10 points; if the bid was 2, each trick is worth 20 points; and so on up to 70 points for a bid of 7.

The scores for each team are recorded on the score sheet below the line, that is, under the heavy horizontal line. *For example, one team takes the bid at 2—in hearts. They capture 9 tricks and score 20 points for each, for a total of 180 points. The other team scores 80 points for 4 tricks. The scorekeeper records these under the line—with his team's score on the We side, and the other team's score on the They side.*

Game and Rubber As soon as a team reaches 500 points they announce this and win a game. This usually happens during the play of a hand, so players have to be alert to the score at all times. The hand is played out to the end, but the game belongs to the first team to reach 500, even if the other team ends up with a higher score.

For example, at the beginning of a hand, Team A has a score toward game of 390, while Team B has 460. The hand is being played at 4—in no-trumps so each trick is worth 40 points. Team

B can win by taking 1 trick, but if Team A can take 3 tricks before this, they will win.

When a team wins a game, they get a bonus score of 1000 points, which is entered above the line. A line is drawn under the game scores for both teams, and on the next hand they will start scoring toward another game.

When a team wins their second game, they score a bonus above the line of 2000 points for winning the "rubber." This ends the play, and all the scores (both above and below the line) made by each team are added. The team with the higher total is the winner.

Failing to Make a Bid If a team fails to take as many tricks as they bid, they are penalized 100 times the value of a trick for each trick they are under the bid. This penalty is entered to the opponent's score, above the line. *For example, Team A takes the bid at 4—in spades. They capture only 8 tricks, 2 under their bid. The penalty for each trick is 40 times 100, or 4000. Team B scores 8000 points above the line. For the tricks they won, Team A scores 320 below the line and Team B scores 200.*

Honors When a hand is played with a suit as trumps, there are two kinds of "honors." One set is the A-K-Q-J-10 of trumps and the other is the 4 aces. The ace of trumps thus is an honor in both sets. The team that holds a majority in a set scores for each card they have in that set. The value depends on the amount of the bid and is 10 times the value of a trick.

For example, Team A takes the bid at 2—in diamonds. Between them they hold the ♠A, ♣A, ◊A, ◊K, ◊J, ◊10. They score for their 3 aces and for their 4 trump honors for a total of 7 honors. The value of a trick is 20, making the value of an honor 200, so they score 1400 points above the line.

In another example, Team A takes the bid at 3—in spades. They hold ♡A, ♠K, ♠Q, ♠J, ♠10. They are ahead in trump honors with 4. Team B's 3 for aces is deducted from this, leaving 1. Team A scores 300 points above the line.

When the aces are split 2 and 2, only the team that wins a majority of the tricks scores for them. A note is made of each team's holdings of honors; and when the play of the hand is completed, the honor score is calculated.

When a hand is played at no-trumps, only the aces are honors. If one team holds 3 or 4 aces, they score 25 times the trick value for each one, above the line. *For example, Team A takes the bid at 4—in no-trumps and holds all 4 aces. A trick is worth 40, making the value of an honor 1000, so they score 4000 points above the line.* When the aces are split 2 and 2 at no-trumps, neither team scores for honors.

Coronets To score for "coronets" a player must hold all of the cards in his hand. The scores are entered above the line and are in addition to any scores for honors.

Three or four aces is a coronet and scores 500 points.

A sequence of 3 or more cards, from the ace down, is also a coronet. In a trump suit or in all suits when no-trumps is being played, the score is 1000 points plus 1000 points for each additional card in the sequence. *For example, if hearts are trumps, a sequence of ♡A-♡K-♡Q-♡J-♡10 in one hand scores 3000 points.* When there is a trump suit, a coronet in a plain suit scores 500 points plus another 500 points for each additional card.

Slams Winning all 13 tricks is called a "grand slam." Winning 12 tricks is called a "little slam." If a team bids 7 at a suit or at no-trumps, they are bidding a grand slam. If a team bids 6, they are bidding a little slam. The table below gives the bonuses (scored above the line) for making and for bidding a slam.

	POINTS
Little slam, made but not bid	1000
Grand slam, made but not bid	2000
Little slam, bid and made	6000
Little slam bid, grand slam made	7000
Grand slam, made and bid	12,000

If a team bids a grand slam but takes only 12 tricks, they do not receive a bonus for the little slam.

TYZICHA from Russia
Number of players 3.
Difficulty level Hard.
Object To be the high bidder, and then to make the number of

points bid, while watching out for a trump that can change at any time.

The Deck   From a regular deck discard the 8's down to the 2's, leaving 24 cards. The cards rank as follows: A (high), 10, K, Q, J, 9.

All of the cards, except 9's, have a point value as shown:

	POINTS
A	11
10	10
K	4
Q	3
J	2

The Deal   Seven cards are dealt to each player, one at a time. The remaining 3 cards are placed face down on the table to form a "widow."

The Bidding   The player to the dealer's right (which is rather unusual) starts by either bidding 110 or passing. The next bid is by the dealer—who may pass, bid 110 if the first player passed, or raise to 120. Bidding continues with the players in turn raising the bid by 10 points or passing—until only one player remains. Once a player passes he may not reenter the bidding.

If the first two players pass, the third player (the one to the dealer's left) is "forced" and may not pass. He is permitted to make a special bid of 100, but will lose certain privileges if he does. The player, instead, may bid the usual opening of 110.

The Widow   The high bidder (except for one who was forced and bid only 100) turns the widow face up for the other two players to see and then takes them into his hand. The player then chooses any 2 cards from his hand and passes one face up to each opponent. All players now have hands of 8 cards. If after making the exchange the player feels that he can make more points, the player is permitted to raise his bid by an even multiple of 10 points (10, 20, 30, etc.).

A player who was forced and bid only 100 takes the widow but does not expose it. The cards passed to the opponents are also not exposed. The player, however, does not have the privilege of raising the bid above 100.

Conceding   If after making the exchange the high bidder feels that he has no chance of making the required number of points, and also that the opponents have a good chance of making more than 40 points each, the player may concede. The amount of the bid is deducted from the player's score (and he may end up with a minus number). Each opponent adds 40 points to his score.

The Play The high bidder leads first. A player must follow suit if possible. A player must also "head" the trick if possible, that is, play a higher card of the suit led or a higher trump if out of the suit led. The winner of one trick leads next.

Trumps Any player when leading, either at the first trick or after winning a trick, may show a "marriage" (king and queen of the same suit) and lead one of them, declaring that suit as trumps. The player also scores, depending on the suit:

	POINTS
Heart Marriage	100
Diamond Marriage	80
Club Marriage	60
Spade Marriage	40

Later marriages may change the trumps one or more times. (It is a good idea to take the four 2's from the deck of cards and place them in a pile where they can be seen, with the current trump on top.)

If a trump is not declared on the first lead, that trick and any tricks until a trump is declared are played without a trump.

Scoring The high bidder totals his points from counting cards captured in tricks and from marriages. If the total is at least equal to the amount of the final bid, the player adds the amount of the bid to his score. If the total is less than the bid, the player deducts the amount of the bid from his score. Each opponent totals his points and adds them to his score.

Game is 1001 points. A player, however, can only reach this by being a successful high bidder. A player who scores points as an opponent must stop at 1000 points and wait until he takes a bid and makes it.

4
More Games from Europe

These games originated somewhere in Europe, but it is impossible to pin them down to any one country.

WAR
Number of players 2 to 4.
Difficulty level Easy.
Object To win all the cards.
The Deck A regular deck of 52 cards, ranking in the regular order.
The Game for 2 The cards are dealt into two equal piles and, without looking at them, each player places one pile face down before him.

At the same time, the players lift the top card from their pile and place it face up on the table. The higher card wins the battle and the winning player takes both cards and adds them to the bottom of his pile, face down. Continue with another battle, and so on.

When the cards from the two players are the same rank, it is a war. Each player places one card face down on top of his original card and then a second card face up. The higher of these two cards wins the war, and the player playing it puts all six cards on the bottom of his pile. If the cards are again the same rank the war continues, and each player plays another two cards until one wins by playing a higher card. If a player does not have enough cards to complete a war, he loses and the game ends.

The game also ends when one player takes the other player's last card through a battle.

The Game for 3   Any one card is removed from the deck and the remaining 51 cards are dealt into three equal piles. All three players show cards at the same time, and the highest wins the battle.

If two cards tie for high, those two players fight a war and the winner takes all the cards played to the table.

If three cards tie for high, all three players fight a war. If after a war starts two of the three players come up with cards that tie for high, these two continue the war until one wins and takes all the cards played during the war.

When one player loses all his cards, that player is out of the game. The other two continue until one wins by capturing all the cards.

The Game for 4   Play is the same as when 3 play, except that the full deck is used and is dealt into 4 equal piles.

Variation   Instead of dealing piles, the deck is separated into the 4 suits. When 2 play, each player takes 2 suits. When 3 play, each player takes a suit and the fourth suit is not used. When 4 play, each player takes 1 suit. The cards each player takes are shuffled and then placed face down to form their piles.

OLD MAID
Number of players   2 to 8.
Difficulty level   Easy.
Object   To avoid getting stuck with the "old maid."
The Deck   A regular 52-card deck with one queen removed, leaving 51 cards.
The Deal   The cards are dealt one at a time until all are dealt. If some players have one more card than others it doesn't matter.
The Play   The players look at their hands for pairs (such as two aces, two kings, etc.) and discard every pair they find face up on the table before them.

After all the pairs have been discarded, the dealer begins the next part of the game. The player to the left of the dealer holds his cards as a fan, with the back facing the dealer. The dealer takes one of the cards. If it forms a pair with a card he already holds, the pair is discarded. If not, the dealer adds the card to his hand.

The player to the dealer's left, who just had a card removed from his hand, now takes a card from the hand of the player on his left. And so on around the table.

Players who discard all of their cards, drop out and the play continues, skipping them. When the last pair has been formed, one queen will remain—the old maid. The player stuck with the old maid is the loser.

Variation In a spirit of fairness, one king can be removed from the deck. The player stuck with the unpaired king, the "old miser," is now the loser.

AUTHORS

Number of players 3 to 8.

Difficulty level Easy to play, but it takes a good memory to play well.

Object To form "books" of four cards, by asking the right player for the right card.

The Deck The game was originally played with special cards showing famous authors and listing their works. But the game plays just as well with a regular 52-card deck.

The Deal The entire deck is dealt out one at a time. Don't worry if some players have one more card than others.

The Play The player to the left of the dealer starts by asking one of the other players for a particular card. The player must have at least one card of the same rank as the card for which he asks, but may not ask for a card he already holds. If the one asked has the requested card, he surrenders it.

After a successful request, the player continues by making another request to any one of the other players, including the one previously asked. The player's turn continues until he receives a no answer instead of the card. The turn then passes to the player on the left.

For example, George (to the dealer's left) holds the ◇ 7 and asks Irv for the ♣ 7. Irv has the card and passes it to George. George also holds the ♡ J and asks Helen for the ◇ J. Not having it, she says no, ending George's turn. Helen is to George's left and it is now her turn. She holds the ♠7 and asks George for the ♣7. After he passes it to her, she asks George for the ♡7. George says no and her turn ends.

When a player collects four cards of the same rank, he shows them and puts them on the table before him as a book. (If a player is dealt a book at the start of the hand, this is shown and put down at once.)

When all of the books have been formed, the play ends.

Scoring The number of books that each player formed is entered on the scoresheet. New hands are played until each player has had a chance to deal. The player with the highest total is the winner. In case of a tie, all players play another hand.

Variation When fewer than 6 are playing, the players may agree to discard one or more of the ranks—such as the 2's, 3's, 4's—to cut down on the size of the hands.

HEARTS
Number of players 3 to 7.
Difficulty level Easy rules, but playing well can be tricky.
Object To avoid taking hearts in tricks.
The Deck From a regular 52-card deck eliminate, depending on how many are playing, the following cards:

NUMBER OF PLAYERS	DISCARD
3	♣2
4	None
5	♣2, ◇2
6	♣2, ◇2, ♠2, ♣3
7	♣2, ◇2, ♠2

The cards rank in the regular order.

The Deal The entire deck is dealt out one at a time. Each player should receive an equal number of cards.

The Play The player to the dealer's left leads with any card. Players must follow suit if able. If not, any card may be thrown. The trick is won by the highest card of the suit led. The winner of one trick leads next. When the hand is completed, each player counts the number of hearts in his tricks.

Scoring Three different methods of scoring are given below. Before the game begins, the players should agree on which one they will use. And, of course, there is nothing to stop the players from coming up with a variation of their own.

Sweepstake Each player starts with an equal point value of chips—the more, the better. But if a player runs out of chips, he simply borrows from a player who is ahead. When the game is finished, unpaid debts are taken into consideration in totaling the points.

At the end of a hand, each player places one point into a pool for each heart he was forced to take. If only one player is "clear" (took no hearts) that player wins the pool. If two or more players are clear, the pool is split between them (any points not dividing evenly are left for the next pool).

If every player was "painted" (took at least one heart) all of the chips remain for the next pool.

If one player took all 13 hearts, that player places 13 points into the pool; but the other players do not collect. Instead, the chips remain for the next pool.

Usually an ending time is agreed upon. When this time is reached, play continues until each player had dealt the same number of times. The player with the most points in chips is the winner.

Howell Settlement At the end of a hand, all players who were forced to take hearts place chips into a pool. For each heart, a player pays as many points as there are players in the game other than himself. (Thus if 5 are playing, each heart costs a player 4 points.)

Then each player collects from the pool a number of points equal to 13 minus the number of hearts with which he was stuck.

For example, in a 5-player game Larry takes 6 hearts and pays 24 points to the pool. Mike, with no hearts, pays nothing. Norma, with 2 hearts, pays 8. Oscar, with 1 heart, pays 4. And Pamela, with 4 hearts, pays 16. Larry takes back 7; Mike takes back 13; Norma takes back 11; Oscar takes back 12; Pamela takes back 9; and the pool is empty.

Agree on an ending time, similar to Sweepstakes.

Cumulative Scoring A running total of the hearts taken by each player is kept on a scoresheet. When one or more players reach an agreed-upon total—such as 50, 75, or 100—the game is ended. The player with the lowest total is the winner. In case of a tie for low, all players play another hand.

BLACK LADY (also known as **BLACK WIDOW** or **BLACK MARIA**).

Number of players 3 to 7.

Difficulty level Easy to learn, but very tricky to play.

Object To avoid taking tricks containing hearts or the queen of spades—or to be daring and try to capture them all.

The Deck and the Deal These are the same as in Hearts.

Passing After looking at their hands, players choose three cards and pass them face down to the player on the left. A player must pass his cards before picking up those passed to him.

The Play This is the same as in Hearts except that, as well as counting the number of hearts taken in tricks, the player taking the queen of spades is also noted.

Scoring Each heart taken scores 1 point, the queen of spades scores 13 points, and a running total is kept of each player's score. If a player takes all 13 hearts and the queen of spades, the player has 26 points deducted from his score (and may end up with a minus score). When one or more players reach a total of 100 points the game is over, and the player with the lowest score is the winner. In case of a tie for low, another hand is played by all the players.

FAN TAN (This is not to be confused with a Chinese gambling game, using soy beans, of the same name. How this game got its name, nobody knows.)

Number of players 3 to 8.

Difficulty level Easy.

Object To get rid of all your cards while stopping the opponents from doing the same with theirs.

The Deck A regular 52-card deck. The cards rank as follows: K (high), Q, J, 10, 9, 8, 7, 6, 5, 4, 3, 2, A (low).

Chips Each player starts with the same point value in chips. It is preferable for the supply to be generous, but if a player runs out of chips, he simply borrows from a player who is doing well. If the loan is not paid back by the end of the game, it is figured in when counting the number of points.

Anteing   Before the deal each player places one point into a pool.

The Deal   The entire deck is dealt one at a time. If some players get one more card than others it doesn't matter.

The Play   Starting with the player to the left of the dealer, each player in turn attempts to play a card from his hand to the center of the table. In each suit, the first card played must be a 7. Once a 7 is down, the 6 and the 8 of the same suit may be played next to it. The 6 may then be covered by the 5, the 5 by the 4, and so on down to the A. The 8 can similarly be covered by the 9, and so on up to the K.

Say for example it is Joan's turn to play, with the situation on the table as shown:

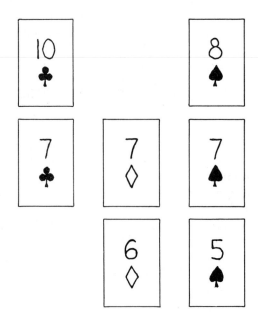

The cards that could be played are ♣J, ♣6, ♢8, ♢5, ♠9, ♠4, or ♡7. If, of these, Joan holds the ♢5 and ♡7, she can choose which one she will play; if she holds only the ♡7, she must play it.

On a turn a player must play one card if able. If not able to play a card, the player passes and adds one point to the pool. The first player to get rid of all his cards wins the pool.

Ending the Game   New hands are played until an agreed time for ending the game is reached. The player who has the most points in chips is the winner.

EIGHTS   (also known as **CRAZY EIGHTS**).

Number of players   2 to 4.

Difficulty level   Easy, but the better player will usually come out ahead, especially when only 2 are playing.

Object   To be the first to get rid of all your cards or, failing that, to have as few points left as possible.

Partnerships   When 4 play, each can play for himself or they can divide into two teams—either by choice or by cutting cards, the two high cards playing against the two low. Partners are seated across from each other.

The Deck   A regular deck of 52 cards.

The Deal   When 2 are playing, 7 cards are dealt to each player, one at a time. When 3 or 4 are playing, each gets only 5 cards. The next card is turned face up in the center of the table and is called the "starter." If the card is an 8, however, it is shuffled back into the deck and a new card is turned. The rest of the cards are placed face down next to the starter as a drawing deck.

The Play   The player to the left of the dealer has the first turn. To play he must cover the starter with a card that is either the same suit or the same rank as the starter. Each player in turn must then cover the last card played with one of the same suit or the same rank.

If a player is unable to play a card, he takes cards from the drawing deck until one that can be played is drawn. The player is permitted to draw even if he has a playable card, but the player must end his turn by playing a card if at all possible.

If after the drawing deck is exhausted a player is unable to play a card, the player simply passes his turn.

All eights are wild, and one can be played regardless of the last card on the pile. The player playing the 8 names any suit, and the next card played must be of that suit or another 8.

For example, the starter is the ♢4. Doris, the player to the dealer's left, plays the ♣4. Ed covers with the ♣J. Frank plays the ♡J. Greta could only play the ♠8 but would like to save it for later; instead she takes cards from the drawing deck until she gets the ♡6 and plays it. Ed, with no sixes and no hearts, plays the ♢8 and names clubs as the suit that has to be followed.

The first player or team to get rid of all their cards wins the hand. If after the drawing deck is exhausted all players are unable to play, the hand ends in a "block."

Scoring The winner of a hand scores for all cards the opponents still hold, as follows: 50 points for each 8, 10 points for each picture, 1 point for each ace, the numerical value of all the other cards.

If the hand ends in a block, each player or team counts the point value of the cards still held. When the game is between 2 players or 2 teams, the one with the lower total scores the difference between the two totals. In case of a tie, no one scores. When the game is between 3 players, the one with the lowest total scores the difference between his total and that of each of the opponents. If two players tie for low, they each collect the difference between their total and the third player's. When the game is between 4 players, the scoring is similar to 3 players.

The scores are recorded and new hands are played, with the chance to deal rotating to the left until a winning score is reached.

PLAYERS	WINNING SCORE
2 players or teams	100
3 players	150
4 players	200

In case two or more players or teams tie with a winning score, another hand is played with all players participating.

Variation To stop a player from taking all the cards in the drawing deck and then controlling the play, no more than 3 cards can be drawn on one turn. If the player is not able to play after the third card, he simply passes.

KLONDIKE (also known as **CANFIELD, FASCINATION, TRIANGLE,** or **DEMON PATIENCE**). Klondike and the next four games belong to a family of games called Solitaire in the United States and Patience in England. They are, of course, played all over Europe and in many other parts of the world. This one is probably the best known of all, and to many players it *is* Solitaire or Patience.

Number of players   1.

Difficulty level   Easy to play, but you don't win very often.

Object   To move all the cards onto piles starting with the four aces.

The Deck   A regular 52-card deck. The cards rank as follows: K (high), Q, J, 10, 9, 8, 7, 6, 5, 4, 3, 2, A (low).

The Deal   Deal a row of 7 cards. Then, skipping the card at the left, deal cards to cover 6 of those in the row. Skip the second card at the left and deal 5 more cards, then 4, then 3, then 2, and finally 1 card at the right. There should now be 7 piles, with 1 card in the left-hand pile—up to 7 cards in the right-hand pile.

Turn the top card of each pile face up and replace it on the pile. In a solitaire, a layout of cards such as this is called a "tableau." (When the deal is finished, a tableau could look like the following illustration.)

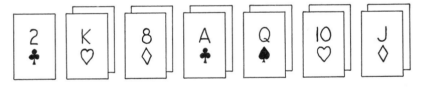

The remainder of the deck is placed face down to form a "stock."

The Play   A card can be moved from one position of the tableau and placed on a card that is the next higher number and a different color. When a card is placed on another, lap them so that the one below is visible. If there is a face-down card under the one that was moved, it is turned face up and becomes available for play. *In the illustration, the ◇J can be moved and placed on the ♠Q. The card exposed by moving the ◇J is turned* *face up. The ♡10 cannot be moved onto the ♢J because they are the same color.*

Two or more cards can be moved together, as long as the one at the bottom can properly be placed in the new position. *Continuing the above example, the ♠Q and ♢J can be moved together and placed on the ♡K.*

As aces become available, they are moved into a row just above the tableau and are called "foundations." Cards of the same suit are placed on a foundation in ascending order—2, 3, 4, 5, up to K. It is not necessary to leave the lower cards visible. *In the illustration, the ♣A is moved above the tableau as a foundation. The ♣2 is placed on it.*

When a space in the tableau is emptied, it can be filled only by a king (and the cards on the king if any). *Continuing the example, when the ♣2 is moved onto the foundation it leaves an empty space. The ♡K, ♠Q, ♢J can be moved together into this space. The game now looks like the following illustration—the ♠4, ♡2, ♣6, and ♢Q were all turned up when the card above was moved.*

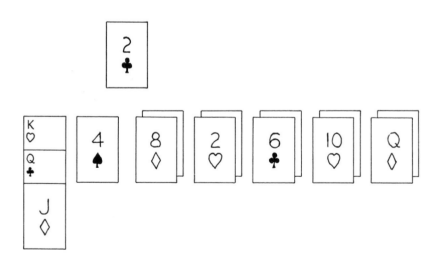

The Stock The top card of the stock is turned. Place it on the tableau or onto the foundation row if possible. If not, place it face up next to the stock to start a "wastepile." Then turn the next card and play it or place it on the wastepile. The card on top of the wastepile is always available.

Continuing the example, the first card from the stock is the ♣4. It can't be played anywhere, so it starts the wastepile. The second card is the ♠2, which is put on top of the ♣4 in the wastepile. The next card turned is the ♠10 which goes onto the ◊J. Next is the ◊5, which goes onto the ♣6; the ♠4 then is moved onto the ◊5, creating a vacant space—but it can't be filled until a king shows. Next from the stock is the ♣3, which goes on the ♣2. Then the ♡3 is turned and goes on the ♠4; the ♠2 on the top of the wastepile is moved onto the ♡3; and the ♣4 which is exposed goes onto the ♣3.

Continue turning the stock. If by the time the stock is completed all the foundations have been filled up to the kings, the game is won. Otherwise the game is lost.

Variation 1 Instead of turning the stock one card at a time, a group of three is lifted (without changing the order) and turned face up next to the stock. If the top card is played, the next one becomes available, etc. Continue turning groups of three cards and placing them on top of the face-up pile. The last group may have less than three cards. When all plays have been made, the face-up pile is turned face down, without shuffling, to form a new stock. Continue in this way until the game is won or until no further plays can be made.

Variation 2 This variation, devised by my father and me, has been played thousands of times with the wins and losses coming out just about even.

Instead of only allowing a vacant space in the tableau to be filled by a king or a column of cards headed by a king, any card or column of cards can be used.

The stock is held in one hand. With the other hand turn a group of three cards face up without changing the order. Only the top card is available for play. The two or three cards (depending on whether one was played or not) are placed face down at the bottom of the stock. Continue until the game is won or until no further plays can be made.

KLONDIKE FOR 2   (also known as **DOUBLE SOLITAIRE**).
Number of players   2.
Difficulty level   Easy.
Object   To move more cards to the foundations than the opponent does.
The Decks   Each player has a regular 52-card deck. The backs should be different so that they can be separated at the end of a game.
The Deal   The players, who are seated facing each other, each deal a tableau as in Klondike. Leave space between the tableaux for two rows of foundations. The player with the higher card at the left end of his tableau plays first. If a tie, the next card decides, etc.
The Play   The play is similar to that in Klondike. Each player uses only his tableau, but once a foundation is in place, either player may place cards on it in proper order.
The Stock   Each player has his own stock. The stock is turned one card at a time (not as in either of the Klondike variations). A player's turn continues until the player places a card turned from his stock onto his wastepile.

When a player ends a turn by placing the last card from his stock onto his wastepile, the wastepile is turned over (without shuffling) to form a new stock.
Forced Plays   Aces must be moved to the foundation rows as soon as they appear. If when a player's turn is over there are one or more cards on his tableau or on top of his wastepile that could be moved to the foundations, the opponent may, but does not have to, force the cards to be moved.
Winning   A player wins by moving all his cards onto the foundations. If the game is blocked, the player with fewer cards remaining in his tableau, stock, and wastepile is the winner. (You'll know that a game is blocked when both players keep going through their stocks without being able to make a play.)

CLOCK
Number of players 1.
Difficulty level Easy.
Object To get all the cards to turn face up.
The Deck A regular deck of 52 cards.
The Deal Deal the cards face down, one at a time, into 13 piles of 4 cards each, as shown.

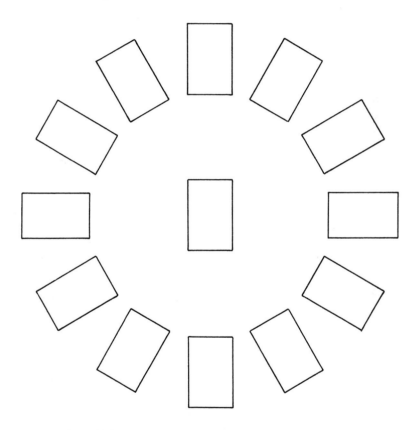

The piles all have numbers. Those around the circle are the same as the numbers on a clock—with 12 at the top, 3 on the right, 6 at the bottom, 9 on the left, etc. The pile in the center is number 13.

The Play   Take the top card from the 13 pile, look at it, and slip it face up under the pile of its own number. (An ace is a 1, a jack is an 11, a queen is a 12, and a king is a 13.) Then take the top card from that pile and similarly slip it under its pile, and so on.

For example, the first card taken from the 13 pile is the ◊6. Slip it face up under the pile in the six o'clock position and take the top card from that pile. If it is the ♣A, it is slipped under the pile in the one o'clock position, etc.

If the last face-down card taken from a pile is the same number as the pile, play continues by taking the next face-down card in a clockwise direction. *For example, you take the last face-down card from the 9 pile and it is the ♡9. You slip it under the pile and are left with four face-up 9's. The 10 pile is also all face up. There is a face-down card on the 11 pile and you continue the game by taking it.*

Winning   You win by turning all the cards face up. If the fourth king is turned while some cards remain face down, you lose.

LA BELLE LOUCIE   (la bell lucy) (also known as **THE FAN, CLOVER LEAF,** and **ALEXANDER THE GREAT**).
Number of players   1.
Difficulty level   Medium.
Object   To free the 4 aces and then pile all the other cards on them.
The Deck   A regular 52-card deck.
The Deal   Deal a "tableau" consisting of 17 "fans" of 3 cards each and a final fan with a single card. (After a deal, the tableau could look like the following illustration.)
The Play   Cards can be moved, one at a time, from the top of one fan to the top of another, if the card moved is of the same suit and one card lower. *For example, in the above illustration the ♣2 (c) could be placed on top of the ♣3 (f). This exposes the ♡4, (c) which could then be placed onto the ♡5 (g), etc.*

When an ace is exposed, it is moved above the tableau and becomes a "foundation." Cards of the same suit are piled onto the foundation, one at a time, in ascending order up to the king. The space left when the last card is played from a fan is never refilled.

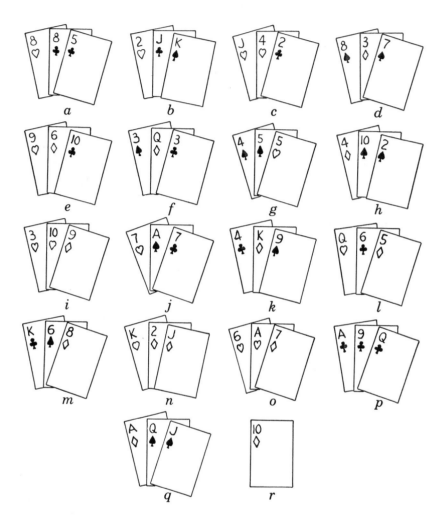

Let's follow the beginning of the game illustrated earlier. The
♢7 (o) could be placed onto the ♢8 (m), freeing the ♡A (o) as a
foundation. However, it is better to place the ♢9 (i) onto the ♢10
(r), the ♢8 (m) onto the ♢9 (i), and then the ♢7 (o) onto the ♢8,
freeing the ♡A (o). Freeing the ♣A (p) takes a little more work.

The ◇ 8 has already been moved from fan m. Place the ♠6 (m) on top of the ♠7 (d), then the ♣Q (p) onto the ♣K (m). Placing the ♣9 (p) onto the ♣10 (e) frees the ♣A. The space emptied when the ♣A is moved cannot be refilled. The ♣2 (c) and then the ♣3 (f) are piled on the ♣A.

Redeals If the play is blocked before all the cards are moved onto the foundations, gather the cards remaining in the tableau, shuffle them, and deal out fans of three cards each. The last fan may have fewer than three cards.

If the play is blocked again, a third and final deal is made in the same way. During this deal the player has a one-time privilege of removing a card from a fan even if it is covered by one or two cards.

Variation To make the game a little easier, allow two or more cards in proper order to be moved from one fan to another. *Using this rule in the illustration above, the ♠Q and ♠J (q) could be moved onto the ♠K (b). The ♠10 and ♠2 (h) could not be moved onto the ♠J (q).*

ACCORDIAN (also known as **IDLE YEAR, METH-USELAH,** and **TOWER OF BABEL**).

Number of players 1.

Difficulty level Easy to play, very hard to win.

Object To get all the cards into one pile.

The Deck A regular 52-card deck.

The Play Deal the cards one at a time, in a row from left to right. A card that is the same suit or the same rank as the card immediately to the left may be moved to cover its neighbor. As cards are formed into piles only the top card counts. If this top card is moved, the ones below are simply carried along. A card may also jump to the left over any two cards if the card landed on is the same suit or the same rank as the one being moved. The gaps formed as cards are moved are filled by shifting the remaining cards to the left.

You are never forced to make an available move. Actually it is usually best to lay out a few more cards in the row to see if something better might come up.

Let's see how this can work. The first 8 cards in the row are as follows:

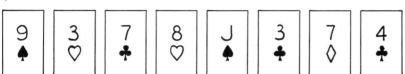

The ♣3 jumps over two cards to land on the ♣7. The ♣3 is then moved onto the ♡3, carrying the ♣7 along below. The ♠J can now jump over two cards to land on the ♠9, etc.

Winning The game is won if all the cards are gathered into one pile.

Variation with Scoring Winning the game with a single pile is extremely difficult, but it is a challenge to see how few piles you can end with. When I play, I take each game as a hole in golf and the number of piles as the number of strokes for that hole. If I can finish 18 holes in 54 or fewer strokes (a par of 3 for each hole), I consider myself a winner.

CALCULATION

Number of players 1.

Difficulty level Easy to learn the rules, but quite tricky to play.

Object To build all the cards into four piles, each pile working in a different order.

The Deck A regular 52-card deck.

Foundations Remove any A, 2, 3, and 4 from the deck and place them in a row on the table. These foundations are to be built up in the order shown below. Only the rank counts, suit is ignored. (Notice that the first foundation is built in increments of one, the second in increments of two, etc.)

FOUNDATIONS —

A, 2, 3, 4, 5, 6, 7, 8, 9, 10, J, Q, K
2, 4, 6, 8, 10, Q, A, 3, 5, 7, 9, J, K
3, 6, 9, Q, 2, 5, 8, J, A, 4, 7, 10, K
4, 8, Q, 3, 7, J, 2, 6, 10, A, 5, 9, K

The Play   After the foundation cards are removed, the remainder of the deck is shuffled and placed face down to form a stock. Cards are turned from the stock one at a time. A card that is the proper rank for one of the foundations is put on that foundation, covering the card below.

A card that can't be placed on a foundation goes to a wastepile. Four wastepiles are formed, generally in a row under the foundations, and you may always choose which one you will use for each card. Although only the top card of a wastepile is available, the cards should be lapped so that the rank of those below is visible in order to plan your play.

When a card at the top of a wastepile is the proper rank for one of the foundations, it is moved to that foundation, and the card below becomes available. A card can never be moved from one wastepile to another. A card may be moved from one foundation to another where it also is the proper rank.

Winning   You win if all four foundations are built up to the kings. You lose if needed cards are blocked beneath others in the wastepiles.

5
Games from the British Isles

WHIST from England. This is the game from which Contract Bridge developed and serves as an excellent introduction. It is also worth playing on its own.

Number of players 4.

Difficulty level Easy, but learning how to cooperate with your partner is an art.

Object To score points by winning tricks and by holding "honors."

The Deck A regular deck of 52 cards, ranking in the regular order.

Partnerships The players are divided into two teams, either by choice or by cutting cards (the two high cards playing against the two low). Partners are seated across from each other.

The Deal Thirteen cards are dealt to each player, one at a time. The last card in the deck is turned face up and sets the trump for the deal. After all players have seen the card, it is picked up by the dealer as part of his hand.

Honors The A, K, Q, and J of the trump suit are known as "honors." Each player makes a mental note of the honors he holds and at the end of the play these will be checked to see if either team scores for honors.

The Play The player to the left of the dealer starts by leading any card. Players must follow suit if able; if not, any card can be thrown. The trick is won by the highest card of the suit led or, if any trumps are played, by the highest trump. The winner of one trick leads next.

Scoring The team winning the majority of the tricks scores 1 point for each trick over 6. (Winning 7 would score 1 point. Winning all 13 would score 7 points.)

If when the cards were dealt one team held all 4 honors, they score 4 points. If one team held 3 honors, they score 2 points. If the honors were divided 2 and 2, neither team scores for honors.

Game and Rubber The first team to score 5 or more points wins a "game," which may take more than one deal.

A team may not win a game by honor points, if they did not also take the majority of tricks in that deal. Instead they must stay at 4 points. *For example, at the start of a deal Team A has a score of 3 and Team B has 1. During the deal Team B takes 8 tricks, adding 2 points to their score, bringing it to 3. Team A held 3 honors but only took 5 tricks so they can't use the 2 points to win; their score goes up to only 4. As another example, a team with no score at the start of a deal takes 9 tricks and holds 3 honors. The 3 points for tricks plus the 2 for honors give them the game.*

If one team takes the majority of tricks and the other team holds 3 or 4 honors, the points for tricks are counted first. If the team scoring for tricks wins a game, the other team does not score for the honors.

The team winning a game earns "rubber points" depending on the opponent's score at the time:

Opponent's Score	Rubber Points
3, 4	1
1, 2	2
0	3

When a team wins their second game, they add a bonus of 2 rubber points to the rubber points for the 2 games. This total is their winning score if the other team did not win a game. If the other team did win a game, the rubber points for that game are subtracted from the total.

Scoring Variations When played in the United States, the scoring is much simpler. Honors are not counted. The first team to reach a score of 7 or more points from tricks is the winner. The opponent's score is subtracted to get the margin of victory.

BLACKOUT   from England.
Number of players   3 to 7.
Difficulty level   Easy and fun.
Object   To announce how many tricks you will take, and then to take exactly that many.
The Deck   A regular 52-card deck, ranking in the regular order.
The Deal   Each game consists of a set number of deals, depending on the number of players:

PLAYERS	DEALS
3	15
4	13
5	10
6	8
7	7

The turn to deal rotates to the left. In the first deal of a game 1 card is dealt to each player. In the second deal, 2 cards are dealt to each, 1 at a time. In the third deal, 3 cards are dealt to each, 1 at a time. And so on, increasing 1 card each deal.

In all deals except the last deal of a game (which is played at no-trump) a card is turned face up to set the trump for that deal. This card and any cards remaining in the deck do not enter the play of the deal.

Bidding   Starting with the player to the left of the dealer, each player in turn bids the number of tricks (from 0 to the number of tricks in the deal) that he expects to take. These bids are recorded by the scorekeeper.

Starting with the fourth deal and for all the rest, the dealer is not permitted to make a bid that makes the total number of tricks bid equal to the number of tricks in the deal. He must instead make a bid that brings the total number of tricks bid above or below the actual number of tricks by at least one.

The Play   The player to the left of the dealer starts by leading any card. Suit must be followed if able, otherwise any card can be thrown. The trick is won by the highest card of the suit led or, if a plain suit lead is trumped, by the highest trump. The winner of one trick leads next.

Scoring A player who doesn't succeed in his bid receives no score. A player who bids 0 and takes no tricks scores 5 points plus the number of tricks in that deal. A player who bids 1 or more tricks and takes the exact amount scores 10 points plus the amount of the bid.

The player with the highest total score after the last deal is the winner. In case of a tie, the tying players share the victory.

CRIBBAGE from England. The invention of this game is credited to Sir John Suckling, a soldier and poet who lived at the beginning of the seventeenth century.

Number of players 2.

Difficulty level Rather hard.

Object To score points in a lot of different ways.

The Deck A regular 52-card deck. The cards rank in the following order: K, Q, J, 10, 9, 8, 7, 6, 5, 4, 3, 2, A. In the play the cards have a counting value as follows: aces, 1; pictures, 10; other cards, their numerical value.

Scoring Device Score is usually kept on a "cribbage board" by moving pegs along rows of holes. If one is not available, chips can be used as a substitute.

You'll need 20 blue chips (10 points), 6 red chips (5 points), and 10 white chips (1 point). These are piled between the players at the start of the game. As scores are made, players take the proper number of points from the piles.

The Deal Six cards are dealt to each player, one at a time.

The Crib Each player secretly chooses 2 cards from his hand and places them face down next to the dealer. This four-card "crib" will be scored by the dealer at the end of the hand.

The Starter The dealer now takes the remaining cards and turns one face up at the top. This is called the "starter," but it actually is not used until later. If, however, the starter is a jack, the dealer scores 2 points at once for "his heels."

The Play Cards are played face up in a row before each player, rather than to the center of the table.

Nondealer starts by playing any card and announcing its count. Dealer then plays a card and announces the total of the 2 cards. Players, in turn, continue until one of the following happens:

1. A player brings the total to exactly 31. He then scores 2 points for a "go."
2. On a player's turn, all the cards in his hand would bring the total over 31. Instead of playing a card, the player says "go." If the opponent can play 1 or more cards without going over 31, he must do so. In any case the opponent scores 1 point for a go, or 2 points if he can bring the total to 31.

For example, Len plays a card that brings the total to 26. Mary has a 7 and a Q in her hand and says "go." If Len holds a 6 and a 10, he cannot play further but still scores 1 point for a go. If he holds a 3, A, 9 he plays the first two (bringing the total to 30) and scores 1 point for a go. If he holds a 5, he plays it, brings the total to 31, and scores 2 points.

After a go, the player who did not score plays a card and starts a new count from zero. The player playing the last card in a hand always scores 1 point for a go or 2 points if it happens to bring the total to 31.

Combinations in Play   Players can score for making any of the following combinations during the play of the hand.

Fifteen—for bringing the total to exactly 15, score 2 points.

Pair—for playing a card of the same rank as the one just played, score 2 points. For playing the third card of the same rank, score 6 points. For playing the fourth card of the same rank, score 12 points.

Run—for playing a card that forms a sequence of three or more cards in numerical order, score as many points as there are cards in the sequence. It is not necessary that the cards are played in sequence. *For example, Len starts by playing a 7, Mary plays a 4, Len continues with a 6, and Mary plays a 5. This forms a sequence of 4-5-6-7 and Mary scores 4 points.*

Let's look at another example of the play of a hand. Len holds 9, 3, 5, Q; Mary holds 3, 3, 4, 2. Len starts with 9. Mary plays a 3, announcing a total of 12. Len plays his 3, bringing the total to 15; he scores 2 points for a fifteen and 2 points for a pair. Mary puts down her second 3, announces a total of 18, and scores 6 points for 3 cards of the same rank. Len (not very wisely) plays his 5, bringing the total to 23. Mary now plays her 4, bringing the total to 27 and scoring 3 points for the sequence 3-4-5. Len can't play his Q, so Mary plays again with her 2; she scores 4 points for the sequence and 1 point for a go. Len plays his Q, the last card of the hand, and scores 1 point for a go.

Scoring a Hand After the play is completed, the hands are scored in this order: 1. nondealer's hand, 2. dealer's hand, 3. dealer's crib. The starter is considered a part of each hand, bringing the number of cards up to 5.

The following combinations in the hands score:

Fifteen—two or more cards that add up to 15 score 2 points.

Pair—two cards of the same rank score 2 points. Three cards of the same rank (known as "pair royal") score 6 points. Four cards of the same rank (known as "double pair royal") score 12 points.

Run—each sequence of 3 or more cards in numerical order scores the number of cards in the sequence.

Flush—all 5 cards of the same suit score 5 points. If the 4 cards exclusive of the starter are the same suit, 4 points are scored. If the starter is the same suit but one of the other 4 cards is not, there is no score for flush.

His nobs—jack of the same suit as the starter scores 1 point.

Each combination that is different by at least one card scores separately. *For example, a hand (including the starter) consists of ◇4, ♠4, ♠5, ♡6, ♣7. Three different fifteens can be formed: ◇4-♠4-♣7, ◇4-♠5-♡6, ◇4- ♠5- ♠6 for a score of 6 points. Two different runs of 4 can be formed: ♠4-♠5-♡6-♣7, ♠4-♠5-♡6-♣7, for a score of 8 points. With 2 points for the pair the total score is 16 points.*

As another example, a hand consists of ♡9, ◇9, ♣9, ◇6, ♠6. Fifteens can be formed in 6 different ways: ♡9-◇6, ♡9-♠6, ◇9-◇6, etc., for a score of 12 points. The 2 points for pair and the 6 points for pair royal bring the score up to 20 points.

Game Points are recorded (on the cribbage board or by chips) as soon as they are scored. New hands are played until a player wins by reaching 121 or more points. (If the game is not won during the play or by turning "his heels," it is important to score the hands in the order listed above. Thus the nondealer may win by just reaching 121 points, even if the dealer could have scored much higher with his hand and crib.) If a player reaches 121 points before the opponent scores 61 points, the opponent is "lurched" and loses a double game.

For a shorter game play to 61 points. The loser is lurched if he fails to reach 31 points.

CASINO   from England.
Number of players   2 to 4.
Difficulty level   Medium.
Object   To use cards from your hand to capture cards on the table.
The Deck   A regular 52-card deck. Aces count as 1's; 2's through 10's count their numerical value. Pictures do not have any numerical value.
Partners   When 4 play they are divided into 2 teams, either by choice or by cutting cards, the 2 high cards playing against the 2 low cards. Partners are seated across from each other.
The Deal   Two cards are dealt to each player, followed by 2 face up on the table. This is repeated a second time. Each player ends up with a 4-card hand and 4 cards are face up on the table.

After the first hands are played, new hands of 4 cards each are dealt to the players, 2 at a time, but no further cards are dealt to the table. Continue in this manner until the deck is exhausted. The dealer announces this by saying "last."
The Play   Starting with the player to the dealer's left, each player in turn plays 1 card from his hand in one of the following ways:

1. *Trailing*—the player simply lays a card face up on the table.
2. *Taking in*—the player uses his card to take one or more cards from the table. A picture card can only take one other of the same kind. (Thus a jack can only take another jack.) A number card can take one or more of the same number and also one or more groups of cards that add up to that number.

For example, the original cards on the table are the two 10's, the ♣7, and the ♡2. One player trails the ♠Q and another the ♢3, leaving the cards on the table as shown.

A player could use any Q to take in the ♠Q. *Any 7 could take in the* ♣7. *A 10 could take in four cards—the* ♣7, ♢3, *and two 10's.*

A player may also take in a "build" that was previously made by himself or by another player (explained later).

3. *Building*—the player adds a card to one or more on the table so that they add up to a card he holds in his hand. *For example, with the table cards as shown above, a player holding a 4 and a 6 could add the 4 to the* ♡2 *and announce "building six." Holding a 2 and a 7, a player could add the 2 to the* ♡2 *and* ♢3 *and announce "building seven."*

A build can be taken in by any player who has the proper card. Other cards can be taken in at the same time. *Continuing the example, if 7 is built, any player with a 7 can take in the build and also the* ♣7.

A card from the table cannot be added to a build in order to take it in. *If the 6 is built as described before, a player cannot add the* ♢3 *to it and take them in with a 9.*

A player who made a build is not permitted to trail while the build he made is still on the table. The player, however, may make any other type of play instead of taking in the build.

4. *Duplicating*—if a player holds two cards of the same number and there is another on the table, the player may play one of the cards onto the table card and announce that he is building that number. *For example, the* ♡5 *is on the table and the player holds two 5's. He plays one onto the* ♡5 *and announces "building fives." This build cannot be taken in by a 10.*

A build on the table can be duplicated in the same way. *For example, a build of 8 is on the table and a player holds two 8's. He adds one to the build and announces "building eights."*

A build on the table can also be duplicated by playing a card from the hand to one or more on the table so that they add up to the amount of the build. The cards are gathered into one pile. *For example, a build of 6 is on the table. A player holds an A and the ◇5 is on the table. The player's A and the ◇5 is added to the build and the player announces "building sixes."*

A build may be duplicated as many times as the cards permit.

5. *Increasing a build*—a player may play a card from his hand onto a build, increasing it to a number that the player holds. *For example, a build of 6 is on the table. A player holds a 3 and a 9. He adds the 3 to the build and announces "building nine."*

A card from the table cannot be used in increasing a build. *In the previous example, if the ◇2 is on the table as well as the build of 6, a player holding an A and a 9 cannot play the A together with the ◇2 to increase the build to 9.*

A player may increase his own build but must hold a card equal to the original build and one equal to the increased build. *For example, a player's hand consists of A, A, 5, 6 and the ♠4 is on the table. The player plays one A and announces "building five." On the next turn he adds the other A and announces "building six."*

A duplicated build may never be increased.

Last Any cards remaining on the table at the end of the final hand belong to the player who was last to take in cards.

Scoring Each player (or team, the partners combining their cards) counts the points taken, as listed in the following table.

	POINTS
Cards, most	3
Spades, most	1
Big casino, the ◇10	2
Little casino, the ♠2	1
Aces, each	1

If no player or team has most of the cards, there is no score for cards. If with 3 players no one has most of spades, there is no score for spades.

Note that the ♠2 scores as little casino and also is counted in determining the majority of spades.

Winning The scores are recorded and new deals are played until a winning score of 21 points is reached. If more than one player or team would reach 21 at the end of a deal, the points are counted in the order given above, starting with "cards." The aces are counted ♠A (first), ♣A, ♡A, ◇A. The first to reach 21 points is the winner.

ROYAL CASINO All the rules are the same as in Casino, except for the following changes: J = 11; Q = 12; K = 13; A = 1 or 14. They can be taken in, built, etc., the same as any other card.

Playing a card that takes in all the cards on the table at that time is a "sweep." (Receiving the remaining cards for "last" is not a sweep.) A record is kept of the order in which sweeps are made and each one scores 1 point. In counting out to see who reaches 21 first, sweeps are counted after all other scores and are counted in the order they were made.

NAP from England (also known as **NAPOLEON**).
Number of players 2 to 6.
Difficulty level Easy.
Object To bid a number of tricks and then to take them.
The Deck A regular deck of 52 cards, ranking in the regular order.
Chips Each player starts with the same point value of chips. Fifty points should be plenty, but if a player runs out, he simply borrows from an opponent who is ahead. At the final counting, any unpaid debts are considered.
The Deal Five cards are dealt to each player, one at a time. The remainder of the deck is out of play for the deal.
Bidding Starting with the player to the left of the dealer, each player in turn has one chance to pass or to bid the number of tricks he contracts to take during the play. The lowest bid is 2; each bid must be higher than the preceding bid. The highest bid is 5 and is called "nap."

If all the players before the dealer pass, the dealer must bid but is permitted to make a bid of 1.
The Play The high bidder names the trump suit and then leads first. Suit must be followed if able, otherwise any card can be thrown. The highest card of the suit led wins the trick unless trumps were played, in which case the highest trump wins. The winner of one trick leads next.

Play stops as soon as the high bidder wins the number of tricks bid or the opponents win enough tricks to stop the bid.
Scoring and Winning If the high bidder makes his bid, he collects as many points as the amount of the bid from each

opponent. If the bid is not made, he pays as many points as the amount bid to each opponent.

A bid of nap (all 5 tricks) is a special case. The high bidder collects 10 points from each opponent if successful, but only pays 5 to each if not successful.

Usually a time is picked to end the game. When this arrives, continue playing until each player has dealt the same number of times. The player with the most points in chips is the winner.

ALL FOURS   from England (also known as **SEVEN-UP**).
Number of players   2 to 4.
Difficulty level   Medium.
Object   To win points by high, low, jack, and game.
The Deck   A regular 52-card deck, ranking in regular order.
Partners   When 4 play they are divided into 2 teams, either by choice or by cutting cards, the 2 high cards against the 2 low. Partners sit across from each other.
The Deal   Six cards are dealt to each player, three at a time. The next card is turned face up to set the first choice for trump suit. If 3 or 4 are playing, only the dealer and the player to the dealer's left look at their cards until this suit is either accepted or rejected.
Choosing Trump   The player to the dealer's left must either "stand" or "beg." If he stands, the suit of the turned card becomes trump, all players pick up their hands, and the play begins.

If the player to the dealer's left "begs," the dealer may insist that the suit of the turned card become trump. For this, the player to the dealer's left gets a "gift" of 1 point. (If this point would cause the player or his team to win the game, the dealer is not permitted to give it.)

If the dealer does not want the suit turned as trumps or does not wish to give away the point, he "refuses gift." The turned card is now discarded, 3 more cards are dealt to each player, and another card is turned. If it is a different suit, that suit becomes trump. If it is the same suit as the card originally turned, it is discarded, another 3 cards are dealt to each player, and another card is turned. Continue until a suit other than the original suit is turned and the game can begin or until the deck is exhausted.

In the latter case the same dealer shuffles all the cards and deals again.

The Play If additional cards were dealt, each player discards enough cards, face down, to reduce his hand to 6 cards. The player to the dealer's left starts by leading any card. Suit must be followed, except that if a plain suit is led, another player may trump it even if he has a card of the suit led. A trick is won by the highest trump or, if no trumps were played, by the highest card of the suit led. The winner of one trick leads next.

Scoring If the original card turned is a jack, the dealer immediately scores 1 point—even if that suit doesn't become trump. If a jack of a different suit is turned later, the dealer scores 1 point. But if the jack of the original suit is turned later, the dealer does not score for it.

After the play, 1 point is scored for each of the following:

High—the highest trump in play. It is scored by the one to whom it was originally dealt.

Low—the lowest trump in play. It is scored by the one to whom it was originally dealt.

Jack—if it is among the cards in play. It is scored by the player taking it in a trick.

Game—the high total of counting cards won in tricks. The counting cards are:

	POINTS
A	4
K	3
Q	2
J	1
10	10

The player or team with the highest count wins the point for game. In case of a tie involving the dealer, the other player or team wins the point. When 3 play and there is a tie for high between the 2 players other than the dealer, there is no score for game.

If there is only one trump in play, it scores for both high and low. If it also happens to be a jack, it scores 3 points. If, as very rarely happens, there are no trumps at all in play, the only score after the play is for game.

Winning The first player or team to reach 7 points wins the game. The dealer may win through the turn of a jack. If after the play more than one player or team is within reach of 7, the points are counted in the order: high, low, jack, and game.

NEWMARKET from England (also known as MICHIGAN, SARATOGA, BOODLE, or CHICAGO).

Number of players 3 to 8.

Difficulty level Easy.

Object To collect from money cards and to play out your hand.

The Deck A regular 52-card deck, ranking in regular order.

You'll also need an ace, king, queen, and jack from another deck—each a different suit—such as ♠A, ♡K, ◇Q, ♣J. These are placed in the center of the table and are known as "money cards."

Chips You'll need a good supply of chips, divided so that each player has an equal point total. If during the game one player runs short, he simply borrows from another player. If a debt can't be paid back when the game ends, it is taken into consideration in counting who has the most points.

Loading the Money Cards Before each deal all players must load the money cards with chips. The dealer places 2 points on each card; the other players place 1 point on each.

The Deal The cards are dealt out one at a time to all the players and to an extra hand, called a "widow," which is directly to the left of the dealer and gets the first card in each round. Some players may end up with one card less than others.

The Widow The dealer may after looking at his hand discard it face down and pick up the widow in its place. If the dealer doesn't wish to make this exchange, he must auction the widow to the highest bidder. That player pays the chips to the dealer and after discarding his own hand takes the widow. Once the exchange is made it is final and may not be reversed. If no player wants the widow it is set aside, still face down.

The Play The player to the left of the dealer starts by placing a card face up before him and announcing the card as it is played. He may choose any suit, but must start with the lowest card held of that suit.

Whoever has the next highest card of the suit played must put it down, announcing its rank. *For example, a player starts with the ♡4, his lowest heart. The player also has the ♡5 and plays it at once. Another player has the ♡6 and puts it down, etc.* Play of a suit continues until it is stopped—either because the next higher card is in the unused hand, the next higher card has already been played, or the ace of the suit is reached.

The player who placed the last card starts a new run by leading the lowest card held of a different suit. If the player doesn't have a different suit, the right to start a new run passes to the left, until a player is reached who has a different suit. If no player has a different suit, play of the deal ends with no "winner." (As a variation, players may agree that when this happens the player placing the last card can start a new run by leading his lowest card of the same suit.)

When a player plays a card corresponding to a money card, the player takes the chips from that card. If no one collects from a money card during a deal the chips remain, but each person still "loads" new chips at the start of the next deal.

When a player gets rid of his last card, play ends and that player is the winner of the deal.

The Payoff The winner of a deal collects 1 point in chips from his opponents for each card remaining in their hands.

Winning the Game A time is chosen for ending the game. When this time is reached, play continues until each player has been the dealer an equal number of times.

If there are chips remaining on any of the money cards, they are distributed. First, each player cuts a card and low cut deals out the cards one at a time. When a player receives a card matching a loaded money card, he collects the chips on that card. Continue until all chips have been collected.

The player with the highest point value of chips is the winner.

SPOIL FIVE from Ireland (also known as **FIVE FINGERS**).
Number of players 3 to 10.
Difficulty level Rather hard, mainly because the cards rank in peculiar ways.
Object To win 3 out of 5 tricks or, failing that, to spoil it for any other player.

The Deck A regular deck of 52 cards.

Rank of the Cards In the trump suit the highest card is the 5, the second highest is the J, and the third highest trump is the ♡A—regardless of which suit is trump. The following table shows this and other differences in the ranking. In actual play not all of the cards will be present, since only part of the deck is dealt out.

RANK OF CARDS IN TRUMP SUITS

♡'s—5, J, A, K, Q, 10, 9, 8, 7, 6, 4, 3, 2.

◇'s—5, J, ♡A, A, K, Q, 10, 9, 8, 7, 6, 4, 3, 2.

♣'s or ♠'s—5, J, ♡A, A, K, Q, 2, 3, 4, 6, 7, 8, 9, 10.

RANK OF CARDS IN PLAIN SUITS

♡'s or ◇'s—K, Q, J, 10, 9, 8, 7, 6, 5, 4, 3, 2, A (◇'s only).

♣'s or ♠'s—K, Q, J, A, 2, 3, 4, 5, 6, 7, 8, 9, 10.

Chips Each player starts with an equal point value in chips. Twenty-five points should be enough, but if a player runs out of chips, he borrows from a rich competitor. At the end of the game unpaid debts are considered in figuring who has the most points.

The Pool At the start of the game each player puts 1 point in chips into a pool. If the pool is not won, only the dealer adds 1 point in the next deal. If the pool is won, all players chip in 1 point to a new pool.

The Deal Each player is dealt 5 cards, either 2 and then 3 at a time, or 3 and then 2. The next card is turned face up to set the trump.

Exchanging If the card turned to set trump is the ace, the dealer can exchange any card in his hand for the ace. The card from his hand is placed face down under the deck without being shown, and the ace is taken into the dealer's hand.

If the ace of trumps is dealt to any player (including the dealer) the player receiving it must announce that he has it at the time he plays to the first trick. At this time the player may (but doesn't have to) secretly exchange any card from his hand for the turned trump.

The Play The player to the dealer's left starts by leading any card. When a plain suit is led and a player has a card of that suit, he must either follow suit or play a trump. If a player does not have a card of the suit led, he may throw any other suit.

When trump is led, a player must follow suit if able; except that the 5 of trumps, the jack of trumps, and the ♡A have a special privilege. A player holding one or more of these cards and no other trumps does not have to follow suit if a lower trump is led. If a higher trump is led, however, suit must be followed. *For example, clubs are trumps. The card led is the ♣J. A player with the ♣5 and no other trump does not have to throw it. A player with the ♡A and no other trump must follow suit by throwing it.*

A trick is won by the highest trump or if no trump is played by the highest card of the suit led. The winner of one trick leads next.

Winning the Pool   To win the pool a player must win 3 of the 5 tricks. If no player succeeds in this, the deal is spoiled and the chips remain for the next deal.

When a player wins his third trick, he can stop playing and collect the pool. If the player wins the first 3 tricks, he can continue playing with the objective of winning all 5. If not successful the deal is spoiled.

If a player is successful in taking all 5 tricks, the player collects the pool and a bonus of 1 point from each of the other players. (As a variation, players may agree to increase the bonus in the following way: The number of points in the pool are counted. Starting with the player to his left, the winner collects 1 point from each player and continues until he gets an amount equal to the number in the pool.)

Ending the Game   The game can be ended by general agreement whenever a pool is won. The player with the highest point total of chips is the winner.

Variation   To make the ranking of the cards easier to follow, the players can agree to change the ranking of the clubs and spades to the same order as that for diamonds. All other rankings remain the same.

SCOTCH WHIST   from Scotland (also known as **CATCH THE TEN**).
Number of players   2 to 7.
Difficulty level   Easy.
Object   To win high trumps in tricks and as many tricks as possible.

The Deck From a regular 52-card deck discard the 5's down to 2's, leaving 36 cards. When 5 or 7 play, further reduce the deck by discarding the ♣6, leaving 35 cards.

The cards rank in the following orders:

Trump suit—J (high), A, K, Q, 10, 9, 8, 7, 6.

Plain suits—A (high), K, Q, J, 10, 9, 8, 7, 6.

Partnerships When 4 or 6 play, each can play for himself or 2 teams can be formed—either by choice or by cutting cards, the high cards against the low. The partners are seated so that the turn to play alternates between the teams.

The Deal The entire deck is dealt out one at a time. The number of cards each player receives is shown below (and has an effect on the scoring).

NUMBER OF PLAYERS	NUMBER OF CARDS
2	18
3	12
4	9
5	7
6	6
7	5

The last card is exposed before the dealer picks it up, setting the trump suit for the deal.

The Play The player to the dealer's left starts by leading any card. Players must follow suit if possible, if not they may throw any card. The trick is won by the highest card of the suit led or if trumped by the highest trump.

The winner of one trick leads next.

Scoring The following high trumps captured in tricks score as shown:

TRUMP	POINTS
J	11
A	4
K	3
Q	2
10	10

Each player or team counts the number of cards taken in tricks and scores 1 point for each card more than the player or team was dealt at the start. *For example, 6 are playing, divided into 2 teams. One team takes 5 tricks for a total of 30 cards. This* is 12 more than the 18 cards originally dealt to them, so they score 12 points for cards. As another example, 5 are playing. Helen takes 2 tricks for 10 cards; she scores 3 points for 3 over her original 7 cards. Irma takes no tricks and scores nothing. John takes 3 tricks for 15 cards and scores 8 points. Karen and Lennie each take 1 trick, but the 5 cards are less than the original 7 so they don't score.

Winning The scores are recorded and new deals are played until a player or team wins by reaching 41 points. If more than one player or team could reach 41 points, the points are counted in the following order to see who wins by getting there first: trump 10, cards, trump A, K, Q, J. For example, in a game between Charles and Deborah, Charles has a score of 29 and Deborah has 30. At the end of the deal Charles has the trump 10, raising his score to 39. Deborah has 6 points for cards, which brings her to 36, and 4 points for the trump ace, which brings her to 40. But Charles has the trump king and wins with a score of 42. Deborah also has the trump queen and jack, but they don't count after Charles wins.

6
Games from Latin America

CONQUIAN (kōn kē' ahn) from Mexico (also known as **COON CAN**). This is one of the earliest of the Rummy games.
Number of players 2.
Difficulty level Medium.
Object To form 11 cards into melds.
The Deck The game was originally played with the Spanish deck of 40 cards, with no 10's, 9's, and 8's. But it is easier to follow if, instead, the picture cards are eliminated from a regular deck leaving 40 cards that rank as follows: 10, 9, 8, 7, 6, 5, 4, 3, 2, A.
The Deal Ten cards are dealt to each player, two at a time. The remainder of the cards are placed face down in the center of the table as a drawing deck.
Melds A meld is a set of 3 or more cards combined in either of the following ways:
Sequence—cards of the same suit that are in numerical order (such as ◇3-◇2-◇A or ♣9-♣8-♣7-♣6-♣5).
Group—cards of the same rank (such as ♠10-◇10-♡10 or ♣4-♡4-◇4-♠4).
The Play The nondealer starts by taking the top card from the drawing deck and placing it face up next to the deck. If he doesn't want this card, he passes. If he picks up this card (as described later), a discard from his hand is put face up in its place.

The dealer now has the chance to pick up the exposed card and discard one from his hand. If not he takes the next card from the drawing deck and places it on top of the exposed card. The dealer then either passes or picks up the card and discards another.

Play continues with each player in turn having a chance to pick up the exposed card or to turn another card and then pass or pick it up.

Picking Up A card that is picked up is never added to the player's hand. Instead, the player puts down cards from his hand to form a meld which remains face up in front of the player. A card can also be picked up to increase a meld already on the table.

For example, Julia has ♡8-♡7-♡6-♡5 in her hand and the exposed card is the ♡4. Julia takes the ♡4 and adds the ♡5 and ♡6 from her hand. She doesn't put down the other two cards of the sequence since she may want to use them in different ways and she can always add them later. At another turn, the ♡3 is exposed. She picks it up to add to the sequence.

Rearranging A player may rearrange his melds so as to allow a card to be picked up, as long as no meld is reduced below 3 cards. *For example, Ken's melds on the table are as shown:*

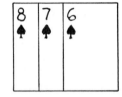

Ken turns the ♡6 from the drawing deck and he has the ◇6 in his hand. He moves the ♠9 from the group to the sequence. This frees the ♠6, allowing a meld of 6's to be formed.

Forcing If a player turns a card face up from the drawing deck that could be added to one of his melds but decides not to do so, the opponent can (but does not have to) force the player to pick up the card. Play continues the same as if the player had picked up voluntarily.

If the card a player faces from the drawing deck could be added to one of the opponent's melds, the player can (but does not have to) force the opponent to pick it up.

When, after picking up, the card discarded from a player's hand could be added to one of the opponent's melds, the player may force the opponent by placing the card on the meld.

Winning A player wins by forming 11 cards into melds. On the player's final turn there is no discard.

If neither player is able to meld 11 cards by the time the drawing deck is exhausted, the game is a draw. The winner of the next game wins a "double." If this too is a draw, the winner of the following game wins a "triple," etc.

PIF PAF (pēf pahf) from Brazil.

Number of players 3 to 8.

Difficulty level The rules of play are rather easy, but knowing how and when to bet is a lot harder.

Object To make the proper bets and then to form 9 cards into melds.

The Deck Combine 2 regular 52-card decks, making 104 cards. The cards rank: K, Q, J, 10, 9, 8, 7, 6, 5, 4, 3, 2, A.

Chips Each player receives an equal point value of chips. The supply should be generous or it will be necessary to keep track of a lot of borrowing. If there are loans that can't be repaid at the time the game ends, they are considered in counting who has the highest point total.

Anteing At the start of each deal all players put 1 point in chips into a pool.

The Deal Each player is dealt 9 cards, one at a time. The remainder of the cards are placed face down in the center of the table as a drawing deck.

Betting After all players look at their hands there is a round of betting, similar to that in Poker. The player to the left of the dealer may bet any number of points up to a "betting limit" equal to the number of players in the game, or the player may pass. If the first player passes, the next player may bet or may also pass. And so on, until a player bets.

After the betting opens, each player may "drop" (withdrawing from the play of the hand), may "stay in" (putting in the points previously bet), or may "raise" (putting in the points previously bet plus any number up to the betting limit). This continues until, after a bet or a raise, all the other players either drop or stay in. If all the players except one drop, that player takes the pool without further play. (For an example of a round of betting see Betting in the game As Nas, page 13. Remember, however, that the betting limit in Pif Paf is higher.)

Some players start with a round of blind betting without looking at the cards. The dealer must put in a bet equal to the number of players in the game. The others in turn may look at their hand and drop or stay in, or without looking may double the last bet. After all players look at their cards, the betting continues with the betting limit equal to the last blind bet. (I don't recommend this way of playing—it's just too wild.)

Melds A "group" consists of from 3 to 6 cards of the same rank. It must contain exactly 3 suits (such as ♠7-♢7-♣7 or ♠J-♠J-♡J-♡J-♢J).

A "sequence" is 3 or more cards of the same suit in numerical order.

The Play The player to the left of the dealer starts by taking the top card from the drawing deck and putting it in his hand. The player then throws out any card from his hand, placing it face up next to the drawing deck to start a discard pile.

Each player in turn has the choice of taking the top card from the discard pile or the top card from the drawing deck. The player then places a card on the discard pile.

A player may claim the top card of the discard pile even if it is not his turn if that card allows him to go out. If more than one player could use a discard to go out, it is taken by the player closest to the left of the player who made the discard.

A player goes out by arranging 9 cards into melds. If no player succeeds in doing this by the time the drawing deck is exhausted, the discard pile is simply turned over (without shuffling) to form a new drawing deck.

When a player has the necessary melds to go out, the player places his discard face down on the discard pile and places his hand face up on the table. The player takes the chips from the pool and, after all players ante, deals the next hand.

Winning A time should be set for ending the game. When this time is reached, the player with the highest point total of chips is the winner.

CANASTA   from Uruguay and Argentina.

Number of players   4.

Difficulty level   Quite hard—there are a lot of things to watch out for.

Object   To score 5000 or more points in various ways, but mainly by forming "canastas."

Partnerships   The players are divided into two teams—either by choice or by cutting cards, the two high cards playing against the two low. Partners are seated across from each other.

The Deck   Two regular 52-card decks with two jokers in each are combined, making a total of 108 cards.

Special Cards   The four jokers and the eight 2's are "wild." They can be used as any card from a 4 up to an A.

The four red 3's are "bonus" cards. The four black 3's are "stop" cards. Both of these will be explained later.

The Deal   Eleven cards are dealt to each player, one at a time. The rest of the cards are placed face down in the center of the table to form a drawing deck.

The top card is turned face up and placed next to the drawing deck to start a discard pile. If this card is a 3 or a wild card, another card is turned, until a card of rank 4 to A is turned. The cards are piled with only the top one showing, except that a red 3 or a wild card is rotated so that it sticks out (as shown in the illustration).

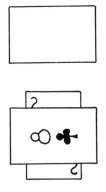

Red 3's   A player finding a red 3 in his hand places it face up on the table before him and takes a replacement from the drawing deck. If during the play a red 3 is drawn, the player puts it down and immediately draws a replacement. If a red 3 was placed in the discard pile at the beginning of a deal, the player taking the discard pile keeps the red 3 face up before him but does not take a replacement.

When play ends, each red 3 has a bonus value of 100 points. But if one team has all four red 3's, the bonus is doubled to 800 points. If a team has put down at least one meld, the bonus is added to their score. If a team has not melded, the bonus is deducted from their score and they can end up with a minus score (below zero).

The Play   The player to the left of the dealer starts, and the turn to play rotates to the left.

A turn consists of the following:

1. *Drawing*—a player may always take the top card from the drawing deck. He may instead take the discard pile (as explained under Taking the Discard Pile).

2. *Melding*—this is optional if the player took a card from the drawing deck. If he took the discard pile, he must meld (again, as explained under Taking the Discard Pile).

3. *Discarding*—a card from the hand (never from a meld on the table) is placed face up on the discard pile.

Melds   A meld consists of 3 or more cards of the same rank. Wild cards—up to a maximum of 3—can be used in a meld, but there must always be at least 2 "natural" cards. *For example, ♠6-♠6-joker-♣2-♡2 is a valid meld. ◇J-joker-♠2 is not valid—only one natural card. ◇9-♠9-♡9-joker-joker-♣2-◇2 is not valid—too many wild cards.*

On his turn a player may meld as many cards as desired—starting new melds and/or adding cards to previous melds. For convenience, all the melds of a team are kept in front of the player who first melded in the deal. A team may meld a rank already melded by the opponents, but may not have two melds of the same rank.

Black 3's can only be melded when a player is "going out" and wild cards may not be used. Thus, the meld can only consist of 3 or 4 black 3's.

Canastas A meld of 7 or more cards is called a canasta. In addition to the point value of the cards in the canasta, it earns a bonus as follows:

Natural canasta—no wild cards—500 points

Mixed canasta—1, 2, or 3 wild cards—300 points

When a canasta is completed, the cards are bunched with a red card on top to indicate a natural or with a black card on top to indicate a mixed. Cards may be added to a completed canasta (by slipping them under the pile) without affecting the bonus, except that a wild card added to a natural canasta reduces it to a mixed. (Remember that a mixed canasta may never have more than 3 wild cards.)

Card Point Values Each card that can be used in a meld has a point value as follows:

	POINTS
Joker	50
2	20
A	20
K, Q, J, 10, 9, 8	10
7, 6, 5, 4, black 3	5

Minimum Count In order to start melding in each deal, one member of a team must lay down one or more melds that meet a minimum point count. This point count depends on the team's score at the beginning of the deal, as follows:

SCORE AT BEGINNING OF DEAL	MINIMUM COUNT
Below 0	15
0 to 1495	50
1500 to 2995	90
3000 or more	120

If the player takes the discard pile, the top card of the pile counts toward the required minimum, but no other cards from the pile can be used for this purpose. Bonuses for red 3's and for canastas cannot be counted.

Once either member of a team has made the necessary starting meld, both players can meld or add to melds without regard to minimum counts.

Taking the Discard Pile The discard pile is "frozen" against a team that has not made its starting meld. If the discard pile contains a red 3, it is frozen against both teams. This can occur only when a red 3 is turned at the beginning of the deal. If the discard pile contains a wild card, it is frozen against both teams. This can occur when a wild card is turned at the beginning of the deal or when one or more players throw wild cards onto the discard pile. (Remember to rotate a wild card so that it sticks out.)

When the discard pile is frozen, a player can take it only by putting down a natural pair from his hand that is the same rank as the top card on the discard pile. This can form a new meld or can be added to a meld already formed by the team.

When the discard pile is not frozen, a player can take it in any of the following ways:

1. By adding the top card to a previous meld.
2. By forming a new meld with the top card, a card of the same rank from the hand, and a wild card from the hand.
3. By forming a new meld with the top card and a natural pair of the same rank from the hand.

After the top card is melded in the proper manner, the player picks up the remainder of the discard pile and adds the cards to his hand. Further melding can take place as desired.

When a wild card or a black 3 is on the top of the discard pile, the pile cannot be taken.

Black 3's When a black 3 is placed on top of the discard pile, it stops the next player from taking the pile. As soon as it is covered it has no further effect—it does not freeze the discard pile.

Black 3's can only be melded when going out. (See Melds.)

Information about Cards Held A player may always ask another player how many cards he holds in his hand. When a player's hand is reduced to 1 card, he must announce this.

Going Out A player goes out by getting rid of all his cards.

The last card may either be melded or thrown on the discard pile. A player may not go out before his team has formed at least one canasta; without this he must keep at least one card in his hand. A player with only one card in his hand may not go out by picking up a discard pile consisting of a single card. When one player goes out, play ends, and the deal is scored. The bonus for going out is 100 points.

Permission to Go Out If after taking a card from the drawing deck but before making any other play a player is able to go out, he may check whether his partner wants him to. The partner's answer must be followed. However, a player may always go out without asking permission.

Concealed Hand In order to go out with a "concealed" hand, a player must on each turn simply take a card from the drawing deck and discard until the player is able to meld his entire hand at one time. (Having picked up one or more red 3's, however, does not stop a concealed hand.) In melding the hand, no cards can be added to melds that his partner may have put down. If the player's partner has not formed a canasta, the concealed hand must contain one.

On the turn the player goes out, he may take the discard pile in the usual manner and must meet the minimum count if his partner has not already made a starting meld. If the player is not able to meld all the cards in the discard pile, he loses the chance to go out with a concealed hand and the game continues.

If on the turn a player goes out he takes a card from the drawing deck, he does not have to meet the minimum count, even if his partner has not melded.

The bonus for going out with a concealed hand is 200 points.

When the Drawing Deck Is Exhausted If the last card taken from the drawing deck is a red 3, it is added to the team's red 3's, but play then stops and the deal is scored. If the last card in the drawing deck is other than a red 3, play continues as long as each player in turn picks up the discard of the previous player.

A player must pick up a discard that matches a meld made by his side (unless the discard pile is frozen or the player holds only one card and there is a single card in the pile). Play ends when the discard is not picked up (unless of course a player goes out in the regular way first).

Scoring a Deal   The bonus scores for each team are determined from the following:

	POINTS
Going out	100
Going out concealed	200
Red 3's (see Red 3's)	
Each natural canasta	500
Each mixed canasta	300

A team's point score is the sum of the point values of all cards melded by the team minus the point values of all cards remaining in the player's hands. (When a player goes out, the cards remaining in his partner's hand are deducted.) A team's score for a deal is the net of its bonus and point scores (and may be a minus).

Game   The scores are recorded on paper, with one column for each team. As a deal is completed, each team's score is entered and totaled with any previous score. This running total sets a team's minimum count for a starting meld.

Game is 5000 points. If at the end of a deal both teams reach 5000, the higher score wins. In case of a tie, play another deal.

Two-Hand Canasta   All the rules apply, except as follows: Each player is dealt 15 cards. When taking from the drawing deck, a player takes 2 cards, but only 1 card is discarded at the end of a turn. A player must have 2 canastas to go out.

Three-Hand Canasta   Three can play exactly the same as 4, except of course that there are no partnerships and each player scores for himself.

A more interesting way for 3 to play is with the following change—each plays for himself, but during the play there are temporary partnerships of 2 against 1.

Drawing   When taking from the drawing deck, a player takes 2 cards, but only 1 card is discarded at the end of a turn.

Lone Hand   The first player to pick up the discard pile becomes the "lone hand." The other 2 players become partners, combining their melds and working together.

If one player goes out before the discard pile is ever picked up, he becomes the lone hand and the other 2 score together (and very often end up with a minus score from all the cards remaining in the 2 hands).

Minimum Count   If 2 players become partners before either has put down a starting meld, the minimum count for each player still depends on his score at the beginning of the deal and can be different.

Drawing Deck Exhausted   If no player goes out, play ends as soon as the player who takes the last card from the drawing deck makes a discard. If the discard pile was never taken during the play, each player scores for himself.

Scoring   Red 3's are scored by each player individually and are not shared by partners. All other scores (both plus and minus) are counted together, and each member of a partnership receives the total. The scores are recorded in 3 separate columns.

Game is 7500 points.

SAMBA   This is a development of Canasta which (from its name) may have started in Brazil. The rules for partnership Samba are the same as for partnership Canasta, except for the following changes and additions.

The Deck   Three regular 52-card decks with 2 jokers in each are combined, making a total of 162 cards.

The Deal   Fifteen cards are dealt to each player, one at a time.

Drawing   When taking from the drawing deck, a player takes two cards, but only one card is discarded at the end of a turn.

Sequences   A meld can consist of 3 or more cards of the same suit in numerical order. For this purpose the cards rank as follows: A, K, Q, J, 10, 9, 8, 7, 6, 5, 4. No wild cards can ever be used in a sequence.

A sequence cannot be longer than 7 cards. At 7 it becomes a sequence canasta—also known as a "samba." (Care should be taken not to put down 2 separate melds that cannot later be joined together to form a sequence canasta, such as 4-5-6 and 9-10-J.)

Canastas   A sequence canasta consists of exactly 7 cards of the same suit in numerical order, with no wild cards. When completed the cards are bunched and turned face down. No cards can be added. It earns a bonus of 1500 points.

A natural canasta is the same as in Canasta. When completed the cards are bunched, with a red card on top. Natural cards of the same rank may be added to the completed canasta, but no wild cards.

A mixed canasta may have 1 or 2 wild cards. (No meld may ever contain more than 2 wild cards.) When completed the cards are bunched, with a black card on top. Natural cards of the same rank may be added to the completed canasta, but no wild cards—even if the canasta contains only one wild card.

Duplicate Melds   A team can put down two separate melds of the same rank, and it is possible to end up with two canastas.

Minimum Count   The minimum count to start melding is as follows:

Score at Beginning of Deal	Minimum Count
Below 0	15
0 to 1495	50
1500 to 2995	90
3000 to 6995	120
7000 or more	150

Taking the Discard Pile   When the discard pile is frozen, a player can take it only by putting down a natural pair from his hand that is the same rank as the top card on the discard pile.

When the discard pile is not frozen, a player can take it in any of the following ways:

1. By adding the top card to a meld of the same rank, but not to a completed canasta.

2. By adding the top card to either end of a sequence on the table, from 3 to 6 cards long.

3. By putting down a natural pair from the hand that is the same rank as the top card.

The discard pile can never be taken as follows:

1. With one card of the same rank as the top card and a wild card.

2. To form a sequence with the top card and 2 or more cards from the hand.

108

Red 3's Each red 3 has a bonus value of 100 points. If one team has all six red 3's, the bonus is 1000 points.

If a team has not formed at least two canastas of any types by the end of the deal, the bonus for red 3's is deducted from their score rather than added.

If there is only one card left in the drawing deck and the player taking it finds that it is a red 3, it is added to the team's red 3's, but play then stops and the deal is scored. If there are only two cards left in the drawing deck and one is a red 3, the play continues in the usual manner.

Black 3's Black 3's are the same as in Canasta, except that the meld of black 3's when going out can contain as many as 6.

Going Out In order to go out a team must have at least two completed canastas of any types.

The bonus for going out is 200 points. There is no extra bonus for going out with a concealed hand.

Scoring a Deal The bonus scores for each team are determined from the following:

	POINTS
Going out	100
Red 3's (see Red 3's)	
Each sequence canasta	1500
Each natural canasta	500
Each mixed canasta	300

Game Game is 10,000 points.

Two-Hand Samba All the rules are the same, except of course that there are no partnerships.

Three-Hand Samba Three can play exactly the same as 4, except of course there are no partnerships and each player scores for himself.

For a more interesting game, the rules for Lone Hand (given in Three-Hand Canasta, page 106) can be added. Game is 15,000 points.

BOLIVIA This is a development of Samba which (from its name) may have started in Bolivia. Except for the following additions and changes, all of the rules are the same as for

Samba. This applies for the partnership game, the 2-hand game, and the 3-hand game—with or without the Lone-Hand rules.

Wild Card Melds and Canastas   Three or more wild cards can be melded. Seven wild cards are a wild-card canasta—usually called a "bolivia." When completed the cards are bunched, with a wild card showing. No further wild cards can be added. A wild-card canasta earns a bonus of 2500 points.

Although wild cards can be melded, the discard pile cannot be picked up when a player has two wild cards in his hand and a wild card is on the top of the pile.

Going Out   In order to go out, a team or player must have at least two completed canastas and at least one must be a sequence canasta (also called an "escalera").

Any two canastas, however, protect a team or player from having the bonus for red 3's deducted.

Black 3's   A black 3 left in a player's hand when any other player goes out scores −100 points. Black 3's melded when going out score 5 points each.

Game   Game is 15,000 points. The minimum count for a starting meld is the same as in Samba.

When 3 play using the Lone-Hand rules, game is 20,000 points.

7
Games from the United States

DRAW POKER Starting in the United States, Poker has spread throughout most of the world and is probably played more than any other card game. Poker, however, is really many games—all closely related to each other, but with considerable differences. I will give you the rules for the two basic games—Draw Poker and Stud Poker—and a fairly simple method of handling the betting (there are many variations). After you master these, you will be ready to search out Spit in the Ocean, Lamebrain Pete, Shotgun, High-Low, and dozens of others.

Number of players 2 to 8.

Difficulty level Can be played at all levels.

Object To get the best possible hand and then to know how to bet on it so as to outsmart your opponents.

The Deck A regular deck of 52 cards, ranking A (high), K, Q, J, 10, 9, 8, 7, 6, 5, 4, 3, 2, A (low only in any "straight" of 5, 4, 3, 2, A).

Rank of the Hands Starting with the highest, the possible Poker hands are:

1. *Royal flush*—the A-K-Q-J-10 of any one suit. All royal flushes are equal.

2. *Straight flush*—five cards of the same suit in sequence. Between two hands with straight flushes, the one headed with the higher card wins. (A royal flush is actually the highest possible straight flush.)

3. *Four of a kind*—four cards of the same rank and any other

card. Between two hands with four of a kind, the higher ranking four of a kind wins.

4. *Full house*—three cards of one rank and two cards of another rank. Between two hands with full houses, the higher ranking three of a kind wins.

5. *Flush*—five cards of the same suit. Between two hands with flushes, the one with the highest card wins. If the highest cards are the same rank, the next highest card governs. If these are the same rank, the next governs, etc. *For example,* $\diamond A$ - $\diamond 6$ - $\diamond 4$ - $\diamond 3$ - $\diamond 2$ *beats* $\spadesuit K$ - $\spadesuit Q$ - $\spadesuit J$ - $\spadesuit 10$ - $\spadesuit 8$. $\clubsuit Q$ - $\clubsuit 9$ - $\clubsuit 8$ - $\clubsuit 6$ - $\clubsuit 3$ *beats* $\heartsuit Q$ - $\heartsuit 9$ - $\heartsuit 8$ - $\heartsuit 6$ - $\heartsuit 2$.

6. *Straight*—five cards of two or more suits in sequence. Between two hands with straights, the one headed with the higher card wins.

7. *Three of a kind*—three cards of the same rank and two unmatched cards. Between two hands with three of a kind, the higher ranking three of a kind wins.

8. *Two pairs*—two cards of one rank, two cards of another rank, and an unmatched fifth card. Between two hands with two pairs, the one with the higher pair wins. If the higher pairs are the same rank, the second pair governs. If these are the same rank, the unmatched card governs.

9. *Pair*—two cards of the same rank and three unmatched cards. Between two hands with one pair, the one with the higher pair wins. If the pairs are the same rank, the highest unmatched card governs. If these are the same rank, the next highest card governs, etc.

10. *High card*—five unmatched cards. Between two such hands, the one with the highest card wins. If the highest cards are the same rank, the next highest card governs. If these are the same rank, the next governs, etc.

Two hands in which the ranks of the cards match each other card for card are tied, since in Poker no suit is higher than another.

Chips Each player starts with an equal point value of chips, the more the better. If a player runs short, he simply borrows from an opponent who is ahead. If a debt can't be repaid, it is considered when counting the points at the end of the game.

THE POKER HANDS

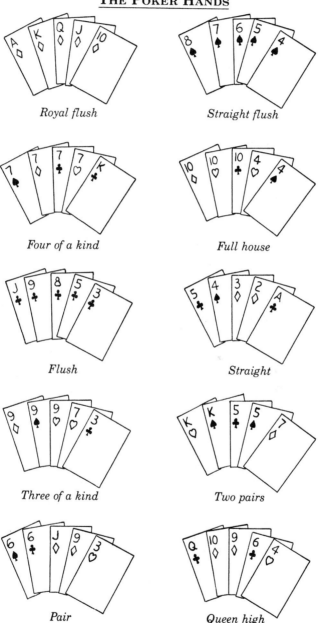

Royal flush

Straight flush

Four of a kind

Full house

Flush

Straight

Three of a kind

Two pairs

Pair

Queen high

The Betting Limit   Before starting the game the players must agree on a "betting limit." This sets the maximum amount that can be bet or raised at any time. Some players allow a bet or raise that is less than the limit; other players make things simpler by keeping all bets and raises to exactly the betting limit. Players must agree on this before starting.

For beginners at Draw Poker I suggest a limit of 2 points before the "draw" (explained later) and 4 points after the draw. I also suggest allowing bets and raises of less than the limit. My explanation of the betting will be based on these suggestions.

The Ante   Before each deal each player puts 2 points into a pool in the center of the table. (This amount, too, can be changed by general agreement.)

The Deal   At the start of the game any player deals out cards face up, one at a time, until a player receives a jack. This player is the dealer for the first hand, and the chance to deal then rotates to the left.

The dealer passes out five cards to each player, one at a time.

The Betting   After the players look at their hands, the betting begins with the player to the left of the dealer. In order to make a bet, the player's hand must contain a pair of jacks or anything better; this is known as having "openers." A player without openers must "pass" (the word "check" is often used in place of pass). A player may pass even if he has openers.

If the first player passes, each player in turn has the same option until one opens the betting. If all players pass, the cards are thrown in and a new hand is dealt by the next dealer. All players ante to the pool again.

Once the betting is opened the next player may:

Drop—placing his hand on the table and withdrawing from the play of the hand.

Stay in (the word "call" is often used in place of stay in)—putting in the points previously bet.

Raise—putting in the points previously bet, plus 1 or 2 more.

This continues until after a bet or a raise all the other players either drop or stay in. (For an example of a round of betting see Betting in the game As Nas, page 13.)

If one player opens the betting and all the others drop, the opening player collects the pool—but must show enough of his hand to prove that he had openers.

The Draw Each player who did not drop during the betting may discard any number of cards from his hand face down before him. The dealer replaces each player's discards, one player at a time, by dealing an equal number from the deck. A player may, if he wishes, keep his original hand (which is known as "standing pat").

If while replacing cards the dealer reaches the bottom card of the deck, this card is not dealt out. Instead, it is added to all the discards and the hands of players who dropped. These are shuffled to form a new deck to continue refilling the player's hands. (The discards of the player who opened the betting should not be taken, so that later he can prove that he had proper openers.)

The Second Round of Betting After the draw, the player who opened in the first round starts the second round by passing or betting. If the original opener dropped during the first round, the active player closest to his left starts. Betting continues until after a bet or a raise all the other players either drop or stay in.

The Showdown All the players who did not drop put their hands face up on the table. The player with the best Poker hand collects all the chips in the pool. In case of a tie, the pool is split, with any odd point going to the player who last bet or raised.

If all players except one drop, that player wins the pool without showing his hand. However, if he was the one who originally started the betting, he must show enough of the hand to prove the openers.

Ending the Game An ending time should be picked in advance. When this time is reached, the game ends when the hand being played is completed. The player with the highest point value in chips is the winner.

STUD POKER

Number of players 2 to 10.

Difficulty level Can be played at all levels.

Object To figure out the strength of the opponents' hands and to fool them on the strength of yours.

The Deck The same as for Draw Poker.

Rank of the Hands The same as for Draw Poker.

Chips The same as for Draw Poker.

The Betting Limit The same as Draw Poker, except for the following: for the first three rounds of betting, a limit of 2 points and for the fourth round of betting, 4 points.

The Ante The same as for Draw Poker.

The Deal At the start of the game any player deals out the cards face up, one at a time, until a player receives a jack. This player is the dealer for the first hand, and the chance to deal then rotates to the left.

One card is dealt to each player face down (called the "hole card"). A second card is dealt to each face up (called an "upcard").

The Betting—First Round After the players look at their hole cards, the betting begins with the player showing the highest ranking upcard. If there is a tie, the tying player closest to the dealer's left begins.

The beginning player must make a bet. After this the betting continues (as in Draw Poker) until after a bet or a raise all the other players either drop or stay in. A player who drops turns his upcard face down.

(For an example of a round of betting, see Betting in the game As Nas, page 13.)

Second Round If two or more players are still "active" (did not drop during the first round), a second upcard is dealt to each active player.

If one or more players have a pair showing, high pair begins the betting. Otherwise, high card governs. In case of a tie, the second card governs, etc.

In this and all following rounds, the beginning player may either bet or pass. The betting then continues in the usual manner. If all players pass there is no betting in a round, but all players remain active.

116

Third Round A third upcard is dealt to each active player. The player who begins the betting is determined by the highest 3 of a kind showing or the highest pair or the highest card, etc.

Fourth Round A fourth upcard is dealt to each active player. The player who begins the betting is determined by the highest 4 of a kind showing or the highest 3 of a kind, etc. Possible straights or flushes are never considered in determining the beginning bettor.

The Showdown After the betting in the fourth round is completed, all of the active players turn their hole cards face up. The player with the best hand collects all the chips in the pool. In case of a tie, the pool is split, with any odd point going to the player who last bet or raised.

If, during any round, all players except one drop, that player wins the pool without exposing his hole card.

Ending the Game The same as for Draw Poker.

PINOCHLE (pē nuk′ l) Although this game is certainly related to Bezique, there are many differences. Pinochle is little known in Europe.

Number of players 2.

Difficulty level Rather hard.

Object To score points by building and declaring melds and by winning counting cards in tricks.

The Deck From two regular decks use the A's down to the 9's, for a total of 48 cards. Special 48-card decks for playing Pinochle are available in stores.

The cards rank A (high), 10, K, Q, J, 9.

All of the cards except 9's have point values:

	POINTS
A	11
10	10
K	4
Q	3
J	2

The Deal Twelve cards are dealt to each player, 3 at a time. The twenty-fifth card is turned face up and sets the trump for the deal. The remainder of the cards are put face down, partially covering the trump card, to form the drawing deck.

If the card turned to set trump is a 9, the dealer scores 10 points. Each player keeps a running total of his own score and the new total is announced each time a player scores.

The Play Nondealer starts by leading any card. While there are still cards remaining in the drawing deck, following suit is not required and any card can be thrown. The trick is won by a trump or by the highest card of the suit led. If two identical cards are played on a trick, the first one played wins.

The winner of a trick takes the top card from the drawing deck and the other player gets the next card. On the final draw, the second player will take the face-up card. The winner of one trick leads next.

Melds The following table shows the various melds, what they are called, and the points scored for making them.

	POINTS
A-K-Q-J-10 of trumps (flush)	150
K and Q of trumps (royal marriage)	40
K and Q of a plain suit (common marriage)	20
♠A-♡A-◇A-♣A (100 aces)	100
♠K-♡K-◇K-♣K (80 kings)	80
♠Q-♡Q-◇Q-♣Q (60 queens)	60
♠J-♡J-◇J-♣J (40 jacks)	40
♠Q and ◇J (pinochle)	40

Scoring Melds Each time a player wins a trick the player may, before taking a card from the drawing deck, declare and score a meld. The meld is placed face up on the table before the player. These cards remain on the table but are still a part of the player's hand and can be played to tricks at any time—including leading a card from a meld directly after scoring the meld.

Only one meld can be declared at a time. *For example, Ronald scored for 80 kings and 40 jacks, and the ♠K and the ◇J are still on the table. He wins a trick and puts down the ♠Q. He can score for either the spade marriage or for the pinochle, but not for both.*

In order to declare a new meld, at least one card must be moved from the player's concealed hand to the table. *Continuing the above example, if Ronald scored for the pinochle, he could not after winning another trick declare the marriage, since both cards are already on the table. If, however, he has another ♠K or ♠Q in his concealed hand, he could put it down and score for the marriage.*

If part of a meld is played in tricks, it cannot be declared again by replacing the missing part from the concealed hand. *For example, Sally scored for the marriage of ♡K and ♡Q and then played the ♡Q to a trick. She cannot declare the marriage again by playing another ♡Q from her concealed hand. If she gets another ♡K and ♡Q in her concealed hand, she can declare and score a second heart marriage.*

If a trump marriage is scored, the A, J, 10 of trump can later be added to score for a flush. If the flush is scored first, the trump marriage cannot be declared later.

There is one exception to the rule that only one meld can be declared at a time. If a player holds a king and queen of each suit in his concealed hand, the player can put all eight cards down at one time, scoring for 80 kings, 60 queens, and the four marriages—a total of 240 points. This is called a "roundhouse."

The 9 of Trumps A player who holds a 9 of trumps can, after winning a trick but before taking a card from the drawing deck, put it down and score 10 points. The player may also declare and score a meld at the same time. If a higher trump card is faced beneath the drawing deck, the player exchanges the 9 for it as well as scoring.

Play of the Last 12 Cards After the drawing deck is exhausted, each player picks up any cards that remain on the table from melds. The play now changes. A player must follow suit if able and must also win the trick if possible by playing a higher card of the suit led or by trumping if out of a plain suit. No melds or 9's of trumps can be scored during this period. The winner of the last trick scores 10 points.

Scoring After play of a hand is completed, each player totals the counting cards he has captured in tricks. These are added to the scores for melds, 9's of trumps, and last trick, and the grand totals are recorded.

New hands are played until a score of 1000 is reached. In case of a tie at 1000 or over, play another hand.

As a variation, some players agree that in order to win, one player must have a score of 1000 or over while the opponent is under 1000. If at the end of a hand both have scores of 1000 or over, the game continues to 1250. If both then have scores of 1250 or over, the game continues to 1500, etc.

CONTRACT BRIDGE This is the aristocrat of card games. Throughout the world, clubs are devoted exclusively to playing it, and serious players gather for tournaments where the competition for "master points" is deadly.

Number of players 4.

Difficulty level The rules are easy, the scoring is harder, and mastering the bidding and the play can take a lifetime.

Object To take the "contract" by bidding the proper amount—not too high and not too low—and then to "make" the bid.

The Deck A regular 52-card deck, ranking in the regular order.

Partnerships Two teams are formed, either by players choosing their own partners or by cutting cards, the two high cards teaming up against the two low. Partners are seated across from each other.

The Deal Thirteen cards are dealt to each player, one at a time. No player should pick up his hand until all the cards are dealt and the dealer is ready to pick up.

Bids When a player bids, he is offering a contract that his team will win a certain minimum number of tricks, with a specified suit as trumps or with no-trump. The number in the bid is not the total number of tricks to be won, but rather the number, of "odd tricks." An odd trick is a trick won after the first 6 tricks which are known as the "book." (Thus, if a player bids 1 no-trump, he is offering a contract to win at least 7 tricks without a trump. A bid of 7 hearts offers a contract to win all 13 tricks with hearts as trump.)

Rank of the Suits In the bidding, the suits and no-trump rank in the following order, with no-trump the highest: no-trump, spades, hearts, diamonds, clubs.

Doubling and Redoubling A player may "double" a bid made by either opponent. If this contract is played, the scoring will be increased (as explained under Scoring), but the number of tricks needed to succeed in the bid is not changed.

Either member of a team that was doubled may "redouble." This further increases the scoring if the contract is played.

The Auction The dealer starts the auction by making any bid or by passing. Each player in turn can either bid or pass. If all 4 players pass, the cards are thrown in and a new hand is dealt by the next dealer.

Once a bid is made, another bid must "overcall" it, that is, name a greater number of odd tricks, a higher suit, or no-trump, or both. *For example, a bid of 1 heart can be overcalled by 1 spade, 1 no-trump, 2 clubs, 2 diamonds, 2 hearts, 2 spades, or any higher bid.* If a player bids and the opponent to his left passes, the bid may be overcalled by the player's partner.

A bid may be doubled by the opponent to the left or, after two passes, by the other opponent. A double can similarly be redoubled by either member of the team originally making the bid. Any overcall by either team wipes out a double or a redouble. (Of course, the new bid can also be doubled.)

After a bid, a double, or a redouble is followed by three passes, the auction is over. The last bid becomes the contract and the team making it are the "contractors." The other team are the "defenders."

The Declarer The member of the contractors who first bid the suit or no-trump of the final contract is the "declarer."

For example, in a game where Gloria and Inez are partners against Harry and Joseph, Gloria starts the auction by bidding 1 club. The bidding then continues as shown:

GLORIA	HARRY	INEZ	JOSEPH
1 ♣	1 ♢	1 ♡	Pass
1 ♠	Pass	1 NT	Pass
2 ♡	Pass	2 ♠	Double
3 NT	Pass	Pass	Double
Pass	Pass	Redouble	Pass
Pass	Pass		

Inez was the first to bid no-trump, so she is the declarer, even though Gloria made the final 3 no-trump bid.

The Play The opponent to the left of the declarer starts by leading any card. As soon as the first lead is made, declarer's partner puts his cards face up on the table before him. Each suit is put in a separate column, lapped so that all cards are visible, with the high card at the top. If there is a trump suit, it is placed so that it is to the declarer's left. This hand is called the "dummy." Declarer plays both hands, but always in their proper turn.

All hands must follow suit if able; if not, any suit can be thrown. The highest card of the suit led wins the trick, unless a plain-suit lead is trumped, in which case the highest trump wins. The winner of one trick leads next.

As a trick is won, the cards are bunched and placed face down in front of the declarer, or in front of one of the opponents. New tricks are lapped so that the number is apparent. When the declarer wins 6 tricks (the book) these are pushed into a single pile and the following tricks are then placed separately.

Scoring The following tables show all the scoring. (How they work will be explained shortly.)

EACH ODD TRICK BID AND WON	UNDOUBLED	DOUBLED	REDOUBLED
Clubs or Diamonds	20	40	80
Hearts or Spades	30	60	120
NT, first odd trick	40	80	160
NT, each odd trick after	30	60	120

These points are entered below the line by the contractors. One hundred points below the line constitute a game.

EACH OVERTRICK	CONTRACTORS NOT VULNERABLE	CONTRACTORS VULNERABLE
Undoubled	Odd Trick Value	Odd Trick Value
Doubled	100	200
Redoubled	200	400
Making doubled contract	50	50

These points are entered above the line by the contractors.

Each Undertrick	Contractors Not Vulnerable	Contractors Vulnerable
Undoubled	50	100
Doubled, first undertrick	100	200
Doubled, each after	200	300
Redoubled, first undertrick	200	400
Redoubled, each after	400	600

These points are entered above the line by the defenders.

Slam Bid and Won	Contractors Not Vulnerable	Contractors Vulnerable
Little slam	500	750
Grand slam	1000	1500

These points are entered above the line by the contractors.

Honors in One Hand	
4 Trump honors	100
5 Trump honors	150
4 Aces at no-trump	150

These points are entered above the line.

Rubber Bonuses	
Two-game rubber	700
Three-game rubber	500
One game in unfinished rubber	300
Part score in unfinished game	50

These points are entered above the line.

The Scoresheet The scoresheet consists of two columns, divided halfway down by a heavy line (see illustration following). The player keeping score enters all scores made by his team under the We column; the opponents' scores go under They.

Game When a team bids a number of odd tricks and makes the number bid or more, they score below the line only for the number bid. Any others are "overtricks."

When a team reaches 100 or more points below the line, they have won a game. A light line is drawn beneath their score and any partial score the other team may have made. Both teams must now start from zero for their next game.

Vulnerability   If a team has not won a game, they are "not vulnerable." Once a team wins a game, they are "vulnerable." This affects various scores, as shown in the scoring tables.

Overtricks   When a team takes more tricks than they bid, the extra tricks are overtricks and are scored above the line.

Making Doubled or Redoubled Contract   When a team is doubled and they make their bid, they get a bonus of 50 points above the line. Redoubling doesn't increase this bonus.

Undertricks   When a team takes fewer tricks than they bid, they are penalized for each "undertrick"—each trick they fall short of the bid. These points are scored by the opponents above the line.

Slams   A bid of 6 is a "little slam" and 12 tricks must be taken to succeed. A bid of 7 is a "grand slam" and all 13 tricks must be taken to succeed. A team bidding a grand slam and taking 12 tricks does not get any credit for a little slam.

Honors   When there is a trump, the A, K, Q, J, and 10 of trump are "honors." When the bid is no-trump, the four aces are honors. To score, the honors must be held in one player's hand. This player announces them after the play of the hand, and his team scores the bonus above the line.

Rubber Bonuses   When a team wins their second game, they score a rubber bonus and the contest is completed. If the other team has not won a game, it is a "two-game rubber." If the other team has won a game, it is a "three-game rubber."

If for some reason the contest is stopped before a rubber is completed, a team gets a bonus if they have won a game and the opponents have not. There is also a bonus for having a partial score toward a game while the opponents do not have any.

Winning   All the points above and below the line are added. The team with the higher total is the winner (not necessarily the team winning the rubber bonus).

Example of Scoring   In the rubber shown, the We team starts by bidding 3 spades and then making 4. Ninety points are scored below the line and another 30 above the line for the overtrick.

WE	THEY
(7) 500	
(6) 100	
(4) 200	
(3) 150	(5) 800
(1) 30	(2) 500
(1) 90	(2) 220
(3) 120	
(6) 60	
(7) 40	
1290	1520

In hand (2) the They team bids 6 no-trump, a little slam. They take all 13 tricks. Technically only 6 odd tricks (or 190 points) should be scored below the line. But since 6 odd tricks score more than enough for game, it doesn't matter if all 7 are scored below the line. For a little slam 500 points is scored above the line.

In hand (3) the We team bids 3 clubs and are doubled. They make 4 odd tricks. The 3 doubled odd tricks are worth 40 points each, for a total of 120 points below the line. The overtrick, since it was doubled (and the contractors are not vulnerable), is worth 100 points. To this is added 50 points for making a doubled contract.

In hand (4) the They team bids 4 hearts but takes only 2 odd tricks. Since the contractors are vulnerable, the opponent scores 100 for each of the two undertricks (200 points above the line).

In hand (5) the We team bids 6 spades and is doubled. They take only 3 odd tricks. Since the contract was doubled (and the contractors are vulnerable) the opponent scores 200 points for

125

the first undertrick and 300 for each of the other two—a total of 800 points above the line.

In hand (6) the We team bids 2 hearts and just makes it. Sixty points are scored toward game. The declarer held $\heartsuit$A- $\heartsuit$Q -$\heartsuit$J -$\heartsuit$10. At the end of the play this is announced and 100 points above the line are scored for honors.

In hand (7) the We team bids 1 no-trump and again just makes it. The 40 points below the line completes the game. The We team scores 500 points for a three-game rubber.

When all the points are totaled, the They team is ahead by 230 points and are the winners.

A Few Words on Point Count In order to reach the proper contract, partners must use their bids to tell each other how strong their hands are. The method most players use for measuring the strength of a hand is "point count."

High cards are given a point value as follows: Each A, 4 points; each K, 3 points; each Q, 2 points; each J, 1 point. There are 40 high-card points in the deck.

These points are modified depending on how the hand is arranged. For instance, if a K, Q, or J is alone or with only one low card in its suit, 1 point is deducted. Holding all four A's adds 1 point; holding no A's deducts 1 point.

Having one suit completely absent adds 3 points to the count. Having only one card in a suit (called a "singleton") adds 2 points. Having two cards in a suit (a "doubleton") adds 1 point. These, however, only count for play with a trump suit.

Each time a player bids he is showing his partner (and the opponents) that the hand contains high points within a certain range. If the partners learn that they have about 26 points, they should usually be able to make a game in no-trump, spades, or hearts. About 29 points is needed for a game in diamonds or clubs. About 33 points will usually make a little slam and 37 points a grand slam.

This, of course, only scratches the surface. But it will give you some idea how fascinating the bidding can become.

RUMMY There are many different variations in the way the game called Rummy is played. This is one of the simplest and a good introduction to the entire Rummy family.

Number of players   2 to 5.

Difficulty level   Quite easy.

Object   To arrange the entire hand into melds.

The Deck   A regular 52-card deck, ranking in the regular order, except that an A can be either at the high or at the low end.

The Deal   The following number of cards are dealt to each player, one at a time:

PLAYERS	CARDS
2	10
3	9
4	7
5	6

The rest of the cards are placed face down in the center of the table as a drawing deck. The top card is turned face up next to the deck to start a discard pile.

Melds   A meld is a set of cards combined in either of the following ways:

Group—3 or 4 cards of the same rank (such as $\diamond$7-$\clubsuit$7-$\spadesuit$7 or $\clubsuit$Q-$\heartsuit$Q-$\diamond$Q-$\spadesuit$Q).

Sequence—3 or more cards of the same suit in numerical order (such as $\diamond$A-$\diamond$K-$\diamond$Q or $\heartsuit$8-$\heartsuit$7-$\heartsuit$6-$\heartsuit$5-$\heartsuit$4 or $\spadesuit$4-$\spadesuit$3-$\spadesuit$2-$\spadesuit$A). An A can be in sequence with a K or with a 2, but not with both. ($\heartsuit$2-$\heartsuit$A-$\heartsuit$K is not a valid meld.)

The same card can never be used in both a group and a sequence. *For example, a player with the following cards:* $\clubsuit$7, $\heartsuit$7, $\diamond$7, $\diamond$6, $\diamond$5 *can form a group of 7's or a diamond sequence, but not both.*

The Play   Starting with the player to the left of the dealer, each player in turn may either pick up the exposed card from the discard pile or take the top card from the drawing deck. He ends the turn by placing a card face up on the discard pile.

Drawing Deck Exhausted   When on a player's turn there are no cards remaining in the drawing deck, the player may take the top card from the discard pile in the usual manner or may turn the discard pile face down (without shuffling) to form a new drawing deck.

Going Out   When after picking up a card a player's hand is completely arranged into melds, the player goes out. His discard is placed face down on the pile and the hand is placed face up on the table.

A player may pick up a card from the discard pile even if it is not his turn if that card will allow him to go out. If more than one player can use a discard to go out, the one closest to the left of the player making the discard gets it.

Each hand is a separate game, won by the player who goes out.

500 RUMMY

Number of players 2 to 4.

Difficulty level Medium.

Object To score points by forming melds.

The Deck The same as for Rummy.

The Deal The following number of cards are dealt, one at a time: 2 players, 10 cards each; 3 or 4 players, 7 cards each. The remainder of the cards are placed face down in the center of the table as a drawing deck. One card is turned face up next to the deck to start a discard pile.

Melds The same as for Rummy.

The Play The player to the left of the dealer plays first. A turn begins with the player picking up one or more cards. The player then can meld as desired and able. The turn ends with a card being placed on the discard pile, lapped so that the card below is visible.

A player may always take the top card from the drawing deck. Or, the player may take any card from the discard pile, as long as that card is melded immediately—either in a new meld using two or more cards from the player's hand, or added to a meld already on the table. If the card was not the top card on the discard pile, the player (after properly melding the card) takes all the cards that cover it into his hand and can meld them as desired.

All the cards a player melds are placed face up on the table before the player. A card can always be added to a meld already on the table, even if the meld is in front of another player. The card, however, remains before the player placing it. *For example,*

128

Anne has a meld of ♠7-♠8-♠9-♠10 in front of her. Ben, on his turn, puts down the ♠J on the table in front of him. Any player may now, on his turn, meld the ♠Q.

If a player puts down a card that could be added to either of two melds, the player announces which meld he chooses. *For example, Anne has the ♠7-♠8-♠9-♠10 in front of her. Ben has the ♡6-♣6-♢6. Carl puts down the ♠6 and announces that he is adding it to the three 6's. The ♠5 cannot now be melded to the ♠6. If Anne had been the player with the ♠6, she also could have chosen to add it to the 6's.*

Ending the Play Play ends when a player gets all of his cards into melds, with or without a final discard.

If no player goes out by the time the drawing deck is exhausted, play continues as long as each player in turn takes one or more cards from the discard pile, melds, and discards. When a player does not take from the discard pile (even if he could) the play ends.

Scoring The cards have scoring values as follows: Ace, 15 points, except when it is in a low sequence (3-2-A) it scores only 1 point; any picture, 10 points; 10 through 2, the numerical value.

When the play is ended, each player totals the values of all cards he has put down in melds. From this the value of all cards still in his hand (even if they could have been melded) is deducted. A player may end up with a minus score (below zero). A player who goes out has no cards to deduct, but gets no further bonus.

Winning Each player's score is recorded and new deals are played until, at the end of a deal, a player has reached a score of 500 points or more. If two or more reach 500, the highest score wins. In case of a tie, all players play another deal.

GIN RUMMY Elwood T. Baker, a Whist teacher from Brooklyn, is credited with having invented this game in 1909. His contribution, undoubtedly, was to put some previous game ideas into a finished form. The game was tremendously popular during the 1940s.

Number of players 2.

Difficulty level The play itself is quite easy, but the better player will win most of the time.

Object Either to form all the cards of a hand into melds, or to "knock" with a few unmatched cards.

The Deck A regular deck of 52 cards, ranking in the following order: K, Q, J, 10, 9, 8, 7, 6, 5, 4, 3, 2, A

The cards have counting values as follows: pictures, 10 points each; aces, 1 point; 2 through 10, the numerical value.

The Deal Ten cards are dealt to each player, one at a time. The twenty-first card is turned face up to start the discard pile. The remainder of the cards are placed face down next to it, to form the drawing deck.

Melds The same as in Rummy, except that an ace can be melded only with a 2 (such as ♠3-♠2-♠A).

The Play The nondealer can start the play by picking up the faced card and then discarding. If nondealer doesn't want the faced card, dealer can start the play by picking it up. If dealer also refuses, nondealer starts by taking a card from the drawing deck.

In turn each player has the choice between taking the card just discarded by the opponent or the top card from the drawing deck. He ends the turn by placing a card on the discard pile.

Going Gin When a player arranges 10 cards into melds, he puts his discard onto the pile face down, places the hand face up on the table, and announces "gin." The opponent puts down all the melds he is able to form. The counting values of the remaining "unmatched" cards are totaled. The player going gin scores the total of the opponent's unmatched cards, plus a bonus of 25 points

Knocking Instead of waiting for gin, a player may "knock" with one or more unmatched cards, as long as their total is 10 points or less. *For example, Sylvia could knock with the following hand: ♡Q-◊Q-♣Q-♠Q, ◊9-◊8-◊7, ♠5, ♠4, ♡A. The three unmatched cards total 10 points.*

When a player knocks, the opponent can form his melds and can also add cards to melds put down by the knocker. *Continuing the above example, if Tom holds the ◊10 he can add it to Sylvia's meld.*

If the opponent's remaining unmatched cards have a higher total than the knocker's total, the knocker scores the difference between the two totals. If the opponent's total of unmatched cards is less than the knocker's total (or possibly can be reduced to 0), the opponent scores the difference between the two totals, plus an "underknock" bonus of 25 points. If both unmatched totals are equal, the opponent scores the 25-point underknock bonus.

Unfinished Hand   The last two cards in the drawing deck may not be taken. If on a player's turn only two cards remain and the player does not wish to take the discard, the hands are thrown in and the same dealer deals new hands.

Scoring   The score is kept in two columns, one for each player. When a score (for gin, knock, or underknock) is entered for a player, a line is drawn under the entry forming a "box."

Sylvia	Tom
(1) 16	(3) 56
(2) 47	

For example, Sylvia knocks on the first hand with 10 points. Tom's unmatched cards total 26 points, so Sylvia scores 16, drawing a line under it. In hand (2) Tom knocks with 6 and Sylvia is able, by adding cards to Tom's melds, to reduce her count to 0. She scores 31 points, which added to the previous 16 gives a total of 47. A line is drawn below this. In hand (3) Tom goes gin and catches Sylvia with 31 points. He enters his 56 points in the box previously formed.

The first player to reach 100 or more points wins the game. He adds a bonus of 100 points to his score. The player with the most boxes adds 25 points to his score for each box he is ahead. *In the previous example, Sylvia would be ahead by one box at this point in the game.*

The lower score is deducted from the higher score to get the margin of victory. (It is possible, though not very usual, for the player who did not get the game bonus to come out ahead because of a lot of box bonuses.)

If a player wins a game before the opponent makes any score, the winner figures his score in the usual manner and then doubles it.

OKLAHOMA GIN   This is exactly the same as Gin Rummy, except that when the twenty-first card is turned up at the start of the game, the count of that card sets the maximum unmatched count a player can knock with. Some players add the rule that when an ace is turned up, a player can only go out with a gin.

Another optional rule that players can agree to use is that when a spade is turned at the start, any score made in that hand is doubled.

8
Something Extra

BURIED TREASURE   is an original game by Ronald Corn
Ronald is a prolific inventor of games, but until now, unfor-
tunately, none were available to the public. Buried Treasure is
an introduction to his novel creations.
Number of players   2 to 8.
Difficulty level   Medium.
Object   To bury a "treasure" consisting of 3 cards, and then to
build up the value of the suits that were buried.
The Deck   When 2 to 5 play, use a regular 52-card deck. When
6 to 8 play, combine two regular decks. The cards from 10 down
to A count as their numerical value, with an ace 1. The pictures
are used in special ways and have no counting value.
The Deal   Eight cards are dealt to each player, one at a time.
The remainder of the deck is placed face down as a drawing deck.
Burying the Treasure   Each player chooses 3 cards and places
them face down before him. Any cards, including pictures, can
be buried, and only the suits will count in determining the value
of the treasure at the end of the play.
The Play   Starting with the player to the left of the dealer,
each player in turn takes a card from the drawing deck and does
one of the following:
1.   Starts a pile by placing a card face up in the center of the
table. (Usually this will be a number card, but there is no rule
against starting with a picture card if the player wishes.)
2.   Adds a card of the same suit to a pile already started.
3.   Removes a card from a pile (as described later).

Four piles of cards are formed, one for each suit. As new cards are added to a pile, they are lapped so that all the cards in the pile are visible.

Protecting a Pile When a player places a picture card of the matching suit onto a pile, the picture card and all cards below it can never be removed. *For example, a pile consists of ♡7, ♡4, ♡10. Nancy, who obviously has at least one heart in her buried treasure, plays the ♡Q onto the pile. None of the 4 cards in the pile can now be touched.*

Removing a Card A player may remove a number card from the top of a pile in either of the following ways:

1.   Playing a picture card of any suit. (With a picture of the same suit, the player can choose whether to remove a card or to protect the pile.)

2.   Playing a number card of any suit that, together with the top card of the pile, adds up to 11. (With a number card of the same suit, the player may instead choose to place the card on the pile, even if the cards add up to 11.)

The card played and the card removed are thrown onto a face-up discard pile.

If a pile consists of a single card, it can still be removed. The pile can be started again by a player playing a card of that suit to the table.

Drawing Deck Exhausted After the player taking the last card from the drawing deck makes his play, each player chooses one of his remaining 5 cards and adds it to his buried treasure. (But see Special Rule for 2 Players.) Play then continues until all of the cards are used.

Special Rule for 2 Players When 2 play, the fourth cards are added to the buried treasures as soon as there are 10 cards placed on the table. Each player then returns his hand to 5 cards by taking a card from the drawing deck, and play continues in the usual manner.

If the players fail to notice when 10 cards are first on the table, the fourth cards are buried as soon as either player points out that there are 10 or more cards on the table. If 10 cards are never reached, the players bury their fourth cards when the drawing deck is exhausted.

Scoring The point value of each suit is determined by totaling the number cards in the pile. *For example, the heart pile consists of ♡7, ♡4, ♡10, ♡Q, ♡A, ♡5. Its point value is 27.* The scorekeeper records the point value for each suit.

The players turn over their buried treasures and are credited with a suit's point value for each card they have of that suit. *Continuing the above example, if Nancy has 3 hearts in her buried treasure, she scores 81 points for hearts. If Oscar has 1 heart in his treasure, he scores 27 points for hearts.*

Winning The scores for a deal are recorded and new deals are played until a player wins by reaching the following score:

2 to 5 players	300 points
5 to 8 players	500 points

If two or more players have reached the winning score, the highest wins. In case of a tie, a new deal is played by all players.

DIVIDE AND CONQUER by Claude Soucie. Claude, too, has invented many games. Among those that have been published are Big Funeral (which is not currently available) and Watch, a fascinatingly simple strategy game for 2 players, from the MPH Games Company.

Number of players 2.

Difficulty level Easy, as long as you know which numbers divide evenly into 12.

Object To outsmart your opponent by picking the card he doesn't expect.

The Cards All you need is one each of the following cards: 2, 3, 4, 5, 6, 7, 8, 9, 10, Q (which is a 12), for a total of 10 cards.

The Deal Five cards are dealt to each player, one at a time.

The Play Each player chooses a card and places it face down before him. After both cards are down, they are turned face up at the same time. This is called a "match" and the winner of a match is determined as follows:

The higher card wins, *unless*

The lower card divides evenly into the higher card, in which case the lower card wins, *or*

The lower card is one number below the higher card, in which case the lower card also wins.

The cards remain face up in front of the players. The winner of a match turns his card so that the short side faces the player; the loser turns his card so that the long side faces him.

For example, after the third match the cards on the table are as shown:

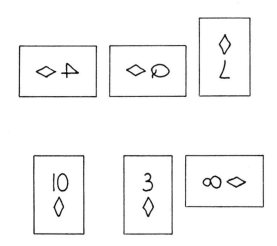

The 10 beats the 4 because it is higher. The 3 beats the Q (12) because it divides evenly into it. The 7 beats the 8 because it is one number below.

Continue until 5 matches have been completed. The number of matches won by each player are recorded. The cards are then exchanged and another 5 matches are played. The player who wins at least 6 of the 10 matches is the winner of the game. If the number is the same, the game is a draw.

Variation For a longer game, use the following cards: 2 through 10 of one suit and 2, 4, 5, 6, 8 of another suit. The cards in the second suit are considered 12, 14, 15, 16, and 18 (and if you don't mind marking up your cards it is easier to follow if you put a 1 in front of each number in a corner). There are now 7 matches in each half of the game. Otherwise, the play is exactly the same.

CARD FOOTBALL   by Sid Sackson.

Number of players   2.

Difficulty level   Fairly easy, but you should know something about football.

Object   To outscore your opponent by knowing when to run, when to pass, or when to kick.

The Deck   A regular 52-card deck. The number cards count as their numerical value, with an ace always a 1. The pictures vary with the different types of plays.

The Field   Although you can keep track of the ball's position just by writing it on a piece of paper, it is a lot easier to follow the game if you make a sketch of the field something like the one shown on an 8½″ × 11″ piece of paper or cardboard. Use a button or any small marker to indicate the exact yard on which the ball is located.

To Start   A coin is tossed and the winner decides whether he will kick off or receive. The player kicking off puts the ball on his 35-yard line. The cards are placed face down between the players.

The Kickoff   The player kicking off turns 3 cards face up from the deck. He then chooses 2 of the 3 and multiplies their values, with a *picture equal to 10*. This is the distance that the ball travels from the player's 35-yard line.

If the player chooses 2 cards of the same suit, the kick is "out of bounds." The player must kick again from the 30-yard line. If again out of bounds, the kick must be from the 25-yard line, etc. *For example, Laura is kicking off and turns ♠Q, ♠8, ♢2. The 80 yards for the 2 spades is out of bounds, but she chooses this rather than the 20 yards she would get from the ♠Q, ♢2. She kicks again from her 30-yard line and turns ♢K, ♣6, ♡4. The ball goes 60 yards and Mike catches it on his 10-yard line.*

When the ball goes to the opponent's goal line (0-yard line) or beyond, the opponent takes possession of the ball on his own 20-yard line. If the ball doesn't reach the goal line, the opponent catches the ball and runs it back. *In the previous example, Mike runs the ball back from his 10-yard line.*

The cards used in all plays are placed in a face-up discard pile.

137

The Runback The player who caught the ball turns cards one at a time. Each number card moves the ball that distance. Continue until a picture is turned, which means that the runner is tackled. The player now has 4 "downs" (chances) in which to move the ball 10 yards toward the opponent's goal line.

If the picture stopping the runback is a club, the runner "fumbles." A coin is tossed and the winner recovers the fumble. The player in possession of the ball now has 4 downs in which to move the ball 10 yards toward the opponent's goal line.

Running The player in possession of the ball announces that he will run, turns a card from the deck, and the result is as follows:

1 through 9 of ♣	Loss of that number
Picture of ♠, ♡, or ◇	Gain of 3 yards
Picture of ♣	Fumble (explained later)
Any 10	Breakaway (explained later)

A fumble is recovered by the winner of a coin toss. If the same player recovers, it is a down with no gain. If the other player recovers, he takes possession of the ball and now has 4 downs in which to move the ball 10 yards toward the opponent's goal line.

With a breakaway, the player continues turning cards until stopped in the same way as in a runback.

Passing The player in possession of the ball announces that he will pass, turns 2 cards from the deck, and the result is as follows:

1. 2 cards of the same color and different numbers—the pass is complete and the gain is found by multiplying the 2 numbers. *For example, Laura calls for a pass and turns ◇3, ♡7. She gains 21 yards.*

2. 2 cards of the same number, regardless of color—the pass is intercepted after traveling a distance found by multiplying the numbers. The player intercepting the pass runs it back in a similar manner to the runback after a kickoff. If the pass is intercepted at the goal line or beyond, the player intercepting takes possession of the ball at his 20-yard line.

For example, Mike is on Laura's 32-yard line. He announces a pass and turns ♣5, ♡5. Laura intercepts the pass on her 7-yard line and then runs back. If Mike, instead, turns ♠8, ♣8 the ball

-10 -10
-9 -8 -7 -6 -5 -4 -3 -2 -1
0 0
1 2 3 4 5 6 7 8 9
10 10
11 12 13 14 15 16 17 18 19
20 20
21 22 23 24 25 26 27 28 29
30 30
31 32 33 34 35 36 37 38 39
40 40
41 42 43 44 45 46 47 48 49
50 50
49 48 47 46 45 44 43 42 41
40 40
39 38 37 36 35 34 33 32 31
30 30
29 28 27 26 25 24 23 22 21
20 20
19 18 17 16 15 14 13 12 11
10 10
9 8 7 6 5 4 3 2 1
0 0
-1 -2 -3 -4 -5 -6 -7 -8 -9
-10

is intercepted past Laura's goal line and Laura takes possession on her 20-yard line.

3. A picture card and a number card of the same suit—the player loses that number of yards. *For example, Laura announces a pass and turns ♣J, ♣7. She loses 7 yards—the passer is tackled behind the line of scrimmage.*

4. Any other combination—the pass is incomplete; the player uses a down with no gain.

First Down If a player (by running and/or by passing) succeeds in moving the ball at least 10 yards in 4 downs or less, the player has made a "first down." He now has 4 more downs to move the ball another 10 yards.

If a player runs and/or passes for 4 downs and fails to gain at least 10 yards, he loses possession of the ball to the opponent.

Punting A player may use one of his downs (usually the fourth one) to kick the ball as far as possible toward the opponent's goal line.

The player announces the "punt" and turns 3 cards from the deck. The movement of the ball is similar to that in The Kickoff, except that a *picture is an 8,* and it is permissible to kick out of bounds. If the ball is kicked out of bounds, the opponent takes possession at the yard line at which it goes out and does not run back.

For example, Mike is on Laura's 44-yard line, with only one down left and 8 yards still to go for a first down. He decides to punt and turns ♠K, ◇6, ◇5. If he chooses ♠K, ◇6, the ball travels 48 yards (past Laura's goal line) and Laura takes possession on her 20-yard line. If he chooses ♠K, ◇5 the ball travels 40 yards; Laura catches it on her 4-yard line and runs back. If he chooses ◇6, ◇5 the ball goes out of bounds on Laura's 14-yard line; she takes possession there, without a runback.

Touchdown A player scores a "touchdown" by running or passing the ball to or past the opponent's goal line. A touchdown scores 6 points. After a touchdown, a player tries for a "conversion" by turning another card. If this is not a picture, the conversion is good and the player scores an additional point. After a touchdown, the player scoring it kicks off from his 35-yard line.

Field Goal A player may use one of his downs to try to kick a "field goal." The player announces the try and turns 3 cards. A 10 or 9 cannot be used. *A picture is a 5.*

The player picks out the 2 highest usable cards and multiplies them. If the result is equal to or greater than the distance to the opponent's goal line plus 10 yards (the goal posts are 10 yards past the goal line), the field goal is successful and the player scores 3 points.

For example, if a player turns ♡10, ♣7, ♡6 the product is 42 and a field goal is successful from the opponent's 32-yard line or closer. If ♠K, ♣J, ◇4 are turned, the product is 25 and a field goal is successful from the opponent's 15-yard line or closer. If ◇9, ♠9, ♡8 are turned, the field goal fails from any position.

After a successful field goal, the player scoring it kicks off from his 35-yard line.

After an unsuccessful field-goal try, the opponent takes possession of the ball on his 20-yard line if the try was made from the 20-yard line or closer. If it was made from farther than the 20-yard line, the opponent takes possession at the position from which the try was made.

Safety If a player is thrown for a loss (either while running or while passing) that brings the player to or behind his goal line, it is a "safety," and the opponent scores 2 points. After a safety, the player who lost the points punts from his 20-yard line.

Quarters A football game is divided into 4 quarters. Once through the deck represents a quarter. If the deck is exhausted while some cards are necessary to complete a play, the discard pile is shuffled and the necessary cards are taken from the top. When this play is completed, all the cards are shuffled and turned to start the next quarter.

At the beginning of the second and fourth quarters, the game continues without interruption. At the beginning of the third quarter, the player who received the ball at the beginning of the first quarter kicks off from his 35-yard line.

Variations For greater realism the following changes can be introduced:

When a pass is completed (see 1 under Passing) or intercepted (see 2 under Passing) and multiplying the 2 numbers would bring it past the opponent's end zone, the numbers are added instead. If this would still bring it past the end zone, the pass is incomplete.

When a kick is caught or a pass is intercepted in a player's end zone, the player has the choice of downing the ball (called a "touchback") and taking possession on his 20-yard line or of running back from the position where the ball is caught.

CARD STOCK MARKET   by Sid Sackson.

Number of players   2 to 6.

Difficulty level   Hard, but not too hard.

Object   To make a profit by buying and selling "stocks" wisely, while trying to make the opponents lose their money.

The Deck   Two regular 52-card decks shuffled together, and 2 jokers that are not used until later in the game.

Chips   You'll need the following number of chips: 40 to 60 white chips—worth $1 each; 20 to 30 red chips—worth $5 each; 20 to 30 blue chips—worth $10 each; 40 to 60 chips of another color or size—worth $50 each. (Play money from a board game, with denominations from $1 to $100, makes an excellent substitute.)

Each player starts with 5 $1 chips, 3 $5 chips, 3 $10 chips, and 3 $50 chips, for a total of $200. The rest of the chips are placed in a "bank." One player is chosen to be the banker who, of course, must keep his chips separate from the bank's.

Information Strip   You'll also need an information strip like the one shown in the illustration that follows. Use a 10″ × 2½″ piece of paper or cardboard.

To Start   Place the information strip in the center of the table. Turn the cards over one at a time. The first number card (an ace is always considered a 1) of each suit is placed face up beneath its space on the information strip. If any picture card or a number card of a suit that has already been placed is turned, the card is put aside. Continue until all four suits have been placed. These are the starting "market values" for the four stocks (suits).

(At the start of a game the market values could be as shown below, with diamonds $7, spades $1, hearts $4, and clubs $6.)

142

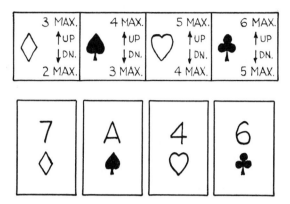

The cards that were put aside are returned and all the cards are reshuffled. Eight cards are then dealt to each player, two at a time. The rest of the cards are put face down as a drawing deck. The player to the left of the dealer plays first.

Buying and Selling Stock A player buys stock by placing a card face up on the table before him. This is the "stock certificate" and the number on the card is the number of shares purchased. The player pays the banker in accordance with the market value of that suit. *For example, Deborah places the ♣3 before her when the market values are as shown in the previous illustration. She pays the banker $18 for 3 shares of clubs stock.*

When a picture is used for buying stock, it is considered a 5. *Continuing the example, if Ernie puts down the ♢Q he buys 5 shares of diamonds and pays $35 to the banker. If he puts down the ♠K he buys 5 shares of spades for $5.*

A player sells stock by removing a stock certificate (card) from the table before him and placing it face up on a discard pile. The banker pays him for the number of shares in accordance with the market value of that suit.

Changing the Market Value A player changes the market value of a stock by covering the card already there with a different card of the same suit. The amount of change must be within the limits indicated on the information strip. *For exam-*

ple, in the illustration above, the market value of diamonds could be raised by covering the ◇7 with a ◇8, a ◇9, or a ◇10. It could be lowered with a ◇6 or a ◇5.

When a picture is used for raising the market value of a stock, a jack is an 11, a queen is a 12, and a king is a 13. *For example, in the illustration above, clubs could be raised to $11 by placing the ♣J. The ♣Q could be used to raise the market value to $12. The ♣K could not be used, since that would raise the value by $7.*

When a picture is used for lowering the market value of a stock, all pictures are a 0. *For example, in the previous illustration, any spade pictures would lower the market value of spades to $0. Any heart picture would lower hearts to $0.*

After a Picture Is Placed When a picture lowers the market value of a stock to $0, the "company" is bankrupt. All players who own shares of that suit place their stock certificates on the discard pile but receive no money from the bank.

When a picture raises the market value of a stock to $11, $12, or $13, the player placing the picture usually sells his stock in that suit, since the price can't go higher. (But he may not be able to sell, as explained later.) Other players with stock in that suit must wait until their turn to sell (and the price may drop before their turn).

When the market value of a suit is a picture, regardless of what value it represented, a player is allowed to place any number card of that suit—but not another picture. *For example, if the market value card for clubs is the ♣Q—representing either $12 or $0—it can be covered by any club from the 10 down to the ace.*

Playing During a Turn Each player in turn may make the following plays:

Place 1 or 2 cards to change market values. If 2 are placed, they can be for different suits or for the same suit.

Sell any number of stock certificates and/or buy 1 or 2 stock certificates. If 2 are bought, they can be for different suits or for the same suit.

A player may make the plays in the order listed above or may make them in the opposite order, selling and/or buying first and

144

then changing the market values. A player may not sell and/or buy both before and after changing the market values. Nor may he change the market values, both before and after buying and/or selling.

For example, Deborah starts her turn by selling all her hearts stock. She then places the ◇9 before her, paying for 9 shares of diamonds. She decides not to buy a second stock certificate. For the other part of her turn she places the ♡J to lower the market value of hearts from $4 to $0 and the ◇10 to raise the value of diamonds from $7 to $10. She cannot now sell or buy any stock. Ernie starts his turn by raising diamonds to $12 by placing the ◇Q on the ◇10. He has only 2 shares of diamonds, so he decides not to sell them. Instead, he places the ◇3 on the ◇Q, lowering the market value to $3. He then puts down the ◇6 and ◇4, buying another 10 shares of diamonds.

A player may decide not to place any cards to change market values, or not to sell or buy any stock. A player may also choose not to make any play, instead throwing off from 1 to 4 cards from his hand to the face-up discard pile.

A player ends his turn by taking enough cards from the drawing deck to return his hand to 8 cards.

Maximum Stock Holdings A player may not own more than 12 shares of any one suit. *For example, Ernie has the ♠K and ♠2 on the table before him for a total of 7 shares of spades. He could not buy the ♠6 since that would raise his holdings to 13 shares. He could buy the ♠3 and ♠A, raising his holdings to 11 shares. He could later buy another ♠A.*

When the Deck Is Exhausted If at the end of a player's turn there are not enough cards in the drawing deck to bring his hand back to 8 cards, the player does not take any until a new drawing deck is formed. All of the market value cards below the top one in each suit are removed and added to the discard pile. Two jokers are also added. All the cards are thoroughly shuffled and then are placed face down as a new drawing deck.

Ending the Game When a player drawing cards at the end of his turn finds a joker, he shows it and the game ends. All players sell their stock certificates at the current market values. The player with the most money is the winner. In case of a tie for most money, the players tying share the victory.

For a Longer Game The players may agree in advance to form one or more drawing decks before adding the jokers.

Bank Out of Money If a player is selling stock and there is not enough money in the bank to pay him, all players must contribute $100 to the bank.

If (as rarely happens) a player does not have $100, he gives all the money he has and pays the remainder when he gets it.

A CATALOG OF SELECTED
DOVER BOOKS
IN ALL FIELDS OF INTEREST

A CATALOG OF SELECTED DOVER
BOOKS IN ALL FIELDS OF INTEREST

CONCERNING THE SPIRITUAL IN ART, Wassily Kandinsky. Pioneering work by father of abstract art. Thoughts on color theory, nature of art. Analysis of earlier masters. 12 illustrations. 80pp. of text. 5⅜ x 8½.   23411-8 Pa. $4.95

ANIMALS: 1,419 Copyright-Free Illustrations of Mammals, Birds, Fish, Insects, etc., Jim Harter (ed.). Clear wood engravings present, in extremely lifelike poses, over 1,000 species of animals. One of the most extensive pictorial sourcebooks of its kind. Captions. Index. 284pp. 9 x 12.   23766-4 Pa. $14.95

CELTIC ART: The Methods of Construction, George Bain. Simple geometric techniques for making Celtic interlacements, spirals, Kells-type initials, animals, humans, etc. Over 500 illustrations. 160pp. 9 x 12. (Available in U.S. only.)   22923-8 Pa. $9.95

AN ATLAS OF ANATOMY FOR ARTISTS, Fritz Schider. Most thorough reference work on art anatomy in the world. Hundreds of illustrations, including selections from works by Vesalius, Leonardo, Goya, Ingres, Michelangelo, others. 593 illustrations. 192pp. 7⅛ x 10¼.   20241-0 Pa. $9.95

CELTIC HAND STROKE-BY-STROKE (Irish Half-Uncial from "The Book of Kells"): An Arthur Baker Calligraphy Manual, Arthur Baker. Complete guide to creating each letter of the alphabet in distinctive Celtic manner. Covers hand position, strokes, pens, inks, paper, more. Illustrated. 48pp. 8¼ x 11.   24336-2 Pa. $3.95

EASY ORIGAMI, John Montroll. Charming collection of 32 projects (hat, cup, pelican, piano, swan, many more) specially designed for the novice origami hobbyist. Clearly illustrated easy-to-follow instructions insure that even beginning papercrafters will achieve successful results. 48pp. 8¼ x 11.   27298-2 Pa. $3.50

THE COMPLETE BOOK OF BIRDHOUSE CONSTRUCTION FOR WOODWORKERS, Scott D. Campbell. Detailed instructions, illustrations, tables. Also data on bird habitat and instinct patterns. Bibliography. 3 tables. 63 illustrations in 15 figures. 48pp. 5¼ x 8½.   24407-5 Pa. $2.50

BLOOMINGDALE'S ILLUSTRATED 1886 CATALOG: Fashions, Dry Goods and Housewares, Bloomingdale Brothers. Famed merchants' extremely rare catalog depicting about 1,700 products: clothing, housewares, firearms, dry goods, jewelry, more. Invaluable for dating, identifying vintage items. Also, copyright-free graphics for artists, designers. Co-published with Henry Ford Museum & Greenfield Village. 160pp. 8¼ x 11.   25780-0 Pa. $12.95

HISTORIC COSTUME IN PICTURES, Braun & Schneider. Over 1,450 costumed figures in clearly detailed engravings—from dawn of civilization to end of 19th century. Captions. Many folk costumes. 256pp. 8⅜ x 11¾.   23150-X Pa. $12.95

STICKLEY CRAFTSMAN FURNITURE CATALOGS, Gustav Stickley and L. & J. G. Stickley. Beautiful, functional furniture in two authentic catalogs from 1910. 594 illustrations, including 277 photos, show settles, rockers, armchairs, reclining chairs, bookcases, desks, tables. 183pp. 6½ x 9¼. 23838-5 Pa. $11.95

AMERICAN LOCOMOTIVES IN HISTORIC PHOTOGRAPHS: 1858 to 1949, Ron Ziel (ed.). A rare collection of 126 meticulously detailed official photographs, called "builder portraits," of American locomotives that majestically chronicle the rise of steam locomotive power in America. Introduction. Detailed captions. xi+ 129pp. 9 x 12. 27393-8 Pa. $13.95

AMERICA'S LIGHTHOUSES: An Illustrated History, Francis Ross Holland, Jr. Delightfully written, profusely illustrated fact-filled survey of over 200 American light-houses since 1716. History, anecdotes, technological advances, more. 240pp. 8 x 10¾. 25576-X Pa. $12.95

TOWARDS A NEW ARCHITECTURE, Le Corbusier. Pioneering manifesto by founder of "International School." Technical and aesthetic theories, views of industry, economics, relation of form to function, "mass-production split" and much more. Profusely illustrated. 320pp. 6⅛ x 9¼. (Available in U.S. only.) 25023-7 Pa. $10.95

HOW THE OTHER HALF LIVES, Jacob Riis. Famous journalistic record, exposing poverty and degradation of New York slums around 1900, by major social reformer. 100 striking and influential photographs. 233pp. 10 x 7⅞. 22012-5 Pa. $11.95

FRUIT KEY AND TWIG KEY TO TREES AND SHRUBS, William M. Harlow. One of the handiest and most widely used identification aids. Fruit key covers 120 deciduous and evergreen species; twig key 160 deciduous species. Easily used. Over 300 photographs. 126pp. 5⅜ x 8½. 20511-8 Pa. $3.95

COMMON BIRD SONGS, Dr. Donald J. Borror. Songs of 60 most common U.S. birds: robins, sparrows, cardinals, bluejays, finches, more—arranged in order of increasing complexity. Up to 9 variations of songs of each species. Cassette and manual 99911-4 $8.95

ORCHIDS AS HOUSE PLANTS, Rebecca Tyson Northen. Grow cattleyas and many other kinds of orchids—in a window, in a case, or under artificial light. 63 illustrations. 148pp. 5⅜ x 8½. 23261-1 Pa. $7.95

MONSTER MAZES, Dave Phillips. Masterful mazes at four levels of difficulty. Avoid deadly perils and evil creatures to find magical treasures. Solutions for all 32 exciting illustrated puzzles. 48pp. 8¼ x 11. 26005-4 Pa. $2.95

MOZART'S DON GIOVANNI (DOVER OPERA LIBRETTO SERIES), Wolfgang Amadeus Mozart. Introduced and translated by Ellen H. Bleiler. Standard Italian libretto, with complete English translation. Convenient and thoroughly portable—an ideal companion for reading along with a recording or the performance itself. Introduction. List of characters. Plot summary. 121pp. 5¼ x 8½. 24944-1 Pa. $3.95

TECHNICAL MANUAL AND DICTIONARY OF CLASSICAL BALLET, Gail Grant. Defines, explains, comments on steps, movements, poses and concepts. 15-page pictorial section. Basic book for student, viewer. 127pp. 5⅜ x 8½. 21843-0 Pa. $4.95

THE CLARINET AND CLARINET PLAYING, David Pino. Lively, comprehensive work features suggestions about technique, musicianship, and musical interpretation, as well as guidelines for teaching, making your own reeds, and preparing for public performance. Includes an intriguing look at clarinet history. "A godsend," *The Clarinet,* Journal of the International Clarinet Society. Appendixes. 7 illus. 320pp. 5⅜ x 8½. 40270-3 Pa. $9.95

HOLLYWOOD GLAMOR PORTRAITS, John Kobal (ed.). 145 photos from 1926-49. Harlow, Gable, Bogart, Bacall; 94 stars in all. Full background on photographers, technical aspects. 160pp. 8⅜ x 11¼. 23352-9 Pa. $12.95

THE ANNOTATED CASEY AT THE BAT: A Collection of Ballads about the Mighty Casey/Third, Revised Edition, Martin Gardner (ed.). Amusing sequels and parodies of one of America's best-loved poems: Casey's Revenge, Why Casey Whiffed, Casey's Sister at the Bat, others. 256pp. 5⅜ x 8½. 28598-7 Pa. $8.95

THE RAVEN AND OTHER FAVORITE POEMS, Edgar Allan Poe. Over 40 of the author's most memorable poems: "The Bells," "Ulalume," "Israfel," "To Helen," "The Conqueror Worm," "Eldorado," "Annabel Lee," many more. Alphabetic lists of titles and first lines. 64pp. 5$\frac{3}{16}$ x 8¼. 26685-0 Pa. $1.00

PERSONAL MEMOIRS OF U. S. GRANT, Ulysses Simpson Grant. Intelligent, deeply moving firsthand account of Civil War campaigns, considered by many the finest military memoirs ever written. Includes letters, historic photographs, maps and more. 528pp. 6⅛ x 9¼. 28587-1 Pa. $12.95

ANCIENT EGYPTIAN MATERIALS AND INDUSTRIES, A. Lucas and J. Harris. Fascinating, comprehensive, thoroughly documented text describes this ancient civilization's vast resources and the processes that incorporated them in daily life, including the use of animal products, building materials, cosmetics, perfumes and incense, fibers, glazed ware, glass and its manufacture, materials used in the mummification process, and much more. 544pp. 6⅛ x 9¼. (Available in U.S. only.) 40446-3 Pa. $16.95

RUSSIAN STORIES/PYCCKNE PACCKA3bl: A Dual-Language Book, edited by Gleb Struve. Twelve tales by such masters as Chekhov, Tolstoy, Dostoevsky, Pushkin, others. Excellent word-for-word English translations on facing pages, plus teaching and study aids, Russian/English vocabulary, biographical/critical introductions, more. 416pp. 5⅜ x 8½. 26244-8 Pa. $9.95

PHILADELPHIA THEN AND NOW: 60 Sites Photographed in the Past and Present, Kenneth Finkel and Susan Oyama. Rare photographs of City Hall, Logan Square, Independence Hall, Betsy Ross House, other landmarks juxtaposed with contemporary views. Captures changing face of historic city. Introduction. Captions. 128pp. 8¼ x 11. 25790-8 Pa. $9.95

AIA ARCHITECTURAL GUIDE TO NASSAU AND SUFFOLK COUNTIES, LONG ISLAND, The American Institute of Architects, Long Island Chapter, and the Society for the Preservation of Long Island Antiquities. Comprehensive, well-researched and generously illustrated volume brings to life over three centuries of Long Island's great architectural heritage. More than 240 photographs with authoritative, extensively detailed captions. 176pp. 8¼ x 11. 26946-9 Pa. $14.95

NORTH AMERICAN INDIAN LIFE: Customs and Traditions of 23 Tribes, Elsie Clews Parsons (ed.). 27 fictionalized essays by noted anthropologists examine religion, customs, government, additional facets of life among the Winnebago, Crow, Zuni, Eskimo, other tribes. 480pp. 6⅛ x 9¼. 27377-6 Pa. $10.95

FRANK LLOYD WRIGHT'S DANA HOUSE, Donald Hoffmann. Pictorial essay of residential masterpiece with over 160 interior and exterior photos, plans, elevations, sketches and studies. 128pp. 9¼ x 10¾. 29120-0 Pa. $14.95

THE MALE AND FEMALE FIGURE IN MOTION: 60 Classic Photographic Sequences, Eadweard Muybridge. 60 true-action photographs of men and women walking, running, climbing, bending, turning, etc., reproduced from rare 19th-century masterpiece. vi + 121pp. 9 x 12. 24745-7 Pa. $12.95

1001 QUESTIONS ANSWERED ABOUT THE SEASHORE, N. J. Berrill and Jacquelyn Berrill. Queries answered about dolphins, sea snails, sponges, starfish, fishes, shore birds, many others. Covers appearance, breeding, growth, feeding, much more. 305pp. 5¼ x 8¼. 23366-9 Pa. $9.95

ATTRACTING BIRDS TO YOUR YARD, William J. Weber. Easy-to-follow guide offers advice on how to attract the greatest diversity of birds: birdhouses, feeders, water and waterers, much more. 96pp. 5³⁄₁₆ x 8¼. 28927-3 Pa. $2.50

MEDICINAL AND OTHER USES OF NORTH AMERICAN PLANTS: A Historical Survey with Special Reference to the Eastern Indian Tribes, Charlotte Erichsen-Brown. Chronological historical citations document 500 years of usage of plants, trees, shrubs native to eastern Canada, northeastern U.S. Also complete identifying information. 343 illustrations. 544pp. 6½ x 9¼. 25951-X Pa. $12.95

STORYBOOK MAZES, Dave Phillips. 23 stories and mazes on two-page spreads: Wizard of Oz, Treasure Island, Robin Hood, etc. Solutions. 64pp. 8¼ x 11. 23628-5 Pa. $2.95

AMERICAN NEGRO SONGS: 230 Folk Songs and Spirituals, Religious and Secular, John W. Work. This authoritative study traces the African influences of songs sung and played by black Americans at work, in church, and as entertainment. The author discusses the lyric significance of such songs as "Swing Low, Sweet Chariot," "John Henry," and others and offers the words and music for 230 songs. Bibliography. Index of Song Titles. 272pp. 6½ x 9¼. 40271-1 Pa. $10.95

MOVIE-STAR PORTRAITS OF THE FORTIES, John Kobal (ed.). 163 glamor, studio photos of 106 stars of the 1940s: Rita Hayworth, Ava Gardner, Marlon Brando, Clark Gable, many more. 176pp. 8⅜ x 11¼. 23546-7 Pa. $14.95

BENCHLEY LOST AND FOUND, Robert Benchley. Finest humor from early 30s, about pet peeves, child psychologists, post office and others. Mostly unavailable elsewhere. 73 illustrations by Peter Arno and others. 183pp. 5⅜ x 8½. 22410-4 Pa. $6.95

YEKL and THE IMPORTED BRIDEGROOM AND OTHER STORIES OF YIDDISH NEW YORK, Abraham Cahan. Film Hester Street based on *Yekl* (1896). Novel, other stories among first about Jewish immigrants on N.Y.'s East Side. 240pp. 5⅜ x 8½. 22427-9 Pa. $7.95

SELECTED POEMS, Walt Whitman. Generous sampling from *Leaves of Grass*. Twenty-four poems include "I Hear America Singing," "Song of the Open Road," "I Sing the Body Electric," "When Lilacs Last in the Dooryard Bloom'd," "O Captain! My Captain!"–all reprinted from an authoritative edition. Lists of titles and first lines. 128pp. 5³⁄₁₆ x 8¼. 26878-0 Pa. $1.00

THE BEST TALES OF HOFFMANN, E. T. A. Hoffmann. 10 of Hoffmann's most important stories: "Nutcracker and the King of Mice," "The Golden Flowerpot," etc. 458pp. 5⅜ x 8½. 21793-0 Pa. $9.95

FROM FETISH TO GOD IN ANCIENT EGYPT, E. A. Wallis Budge. Rich detailed survey of Egyptian conception of "God" and gods, magic, cult of animals, Osiris, more. Also, superb English translations of hymns and legends. 240 illustrations. 545pp. 5⅜ x 8½. 25803-3 Pa. $13.95

FRENCH STORIES/CONTES FRANÇAIS: A Dual-Language Book, Wallace Fowlie. Ten stories by French masters, Voltaire to Camus: "Micromegas" by Voltaire; "The Atheist's Mass" by Balzac; "Minuet" by de Maupassant; "The Guest" by Camus, six more. Excellent English translations on facing pages. Also French-English vocabulary list, exercises, more. 352pp. 5⅜ x 8½. 26443-2 Pa. $9.95

CHICAGO AT THE TURN OF THE CENTURY IN PHOTOGRAPHS: 122 Historic Views from the Collections of the Chicago Historical Society, Larry A. Viskochil. Rare large-format prints offer detailed views of City Hall, State Street, the Loop, Hull House, Union Station, many other landmarks, circa 1904-1913. Introduction. Captions. Maps. 144pp. 9⅜ x 12¼. 24656-6 Pa. $12.95

OLD BROOKLYN IN EARLY PHOTOGRAPHS, 1865-1929, William Lee Younger. Luna Park, Gravesend race track, construction of Grand Army Plaza, moving of Hotel Brighton, etc. 157 previously unpublished photographs. 165pp. 8⅞ x 11¾. 23587-4 Pa. $13.95

THE MYTHS OF THE NORTH AMERICAN INDIANS, Lewis Spence. Rich anthology of the myths and legends of the Algonquins, Iroquois, Pawnees and Sioux, prefaced by an extensive historical and ethnological commentary. 36 illustrations. 480pp. 5⅜ x 8½. 25967-6 Pa. $10.95

AN ENCYCLOPEDIA OF BATTLES: Accounts of Over 1,560 Battles from 1479 B.C. to the Present, David Eggenberger. Essential details of every major battle in recorded history from the first battle of Megiddo in 1479 B.C. to Grenada in 1984. List of Battle Maps. New Appendix covering the years 1967-1984. Index. 99 illustrations. 544pp. 6½ x 9¼. 24913-1 Pa. $16.95

SAILING ALONE AROUND THE WORLD, Captain Joshua Slocum. First man to sail around the world, alone, in small boat. One of great feats of seamanship told in delightful manner. 67 illustrations. 294pp. 5⅜ x 8½. 20326-3 Pa. $6.95

ANARCHISM AND OTHER ESSAYS, Emma Goldman. Powerful, penetrating, prophetic essays on direct action, role of minorities, prison reform, puritan hypocrisy, violence, etc. 271pp. 5⅜ x 8½. 22484-8 Pa. $8.95

MYTHS OF THE HINDUS AND BUDDHISTS, Ananda K. Coomaraswamy and Sister Nivedita. Great stories of the epics; deeds of Krishna, Shiva, taken from puranas, Vedas, folk tales; etc. 32 illustrations. 400pp. 5⅜ x 8½. 21759-0 Pa. $12.95

THE TRAUMA OF BIRTH, Otto Rank. Rank's controversial thesis that anxiety neurosis is caused by profound psychological trauma which occurs at birth. 256pp. 5⅜ x 8½. 27974-X Pa. $7.95

A THEOLOGICO-POLITICAL TREATISE, Benedict Spinoza. Also contains unfinished Political Treatise. Great classic on religious liberty, theory of government on common consent. R. Elwes translation. Total of 421pp. 5⅜ x 8½. 20249-6 Pa. $10.95

MY BONDAGE AND MY FREEDOM, Frederick Douglass. Born a slave, Douglass became outspoken force in antislavery movement. The best of Douglass' autobiographies. Graphic description of slave life. 464pp. 5⅜ x 8½. 22457-0 Pa. $8.95

FOLLOWING THE EQUATOR: A Journey Around the World, Mark Twain. Fascinating humorous account of 1897 voyage to Hawaii, Australia, India, New Zealand, etc. Ironic, bemused reports on peoples, customs, climate, flora and fauna, politics, much more. 197 illustrations. 720pp. 5⅜ x 8½. 26113-1 Pa. $15.95

THE PEOPLE CALLED SHAKERS, Edward D. Andrews. Definitive study of Shakers: origins, beliefs, practices, dances, social organization, furniture and crafts, etc. 33 illustrations. 351pp. 5⅜ x 8½. 21081-2 Pa. $12.95

THE MYTHS OF GREECE AND ROME, H. A. Guerber. A classic of mythology, generously illustrated, long prized for its simple, graphic, accurate retelling of the principal myths of Greece and Rome, and for its commentary on their origins and significance. With 64 illustrations by Michelangelo, Raphael, Titian, Rubens, Canova, Bernini and others. 480pp. 5⅜ x 8½. 27584-1 Pa. $10.95

PSYCHOLOGY OF MUSIC, Carl E. Seashore. Classic work discusses music as a medium from psychological viewpoint. Clear treatment of physical acoustics, auditory apparatus, sound perception, development of musical skills, nature of musical feeling, host of other topics. 88 figures. 408pp. 5⅜ x 8½. 21851-1 Pa. $11.95

THE PHILOSOPHY OF HISTORY, Georg W. Hegel. Great classic of Western thought develops concept that history is not chance but rational process, the evolution of freedom. 457pp. 5⅜ x 8½. 20112-0 Pa. $9.95

THE BOOK OF TEA, Kakuzo Okakura. Minor classic of the Orient: entertaining, charming explanation, interpretation of traditional Japanese culture in terms of tea ceremony. 94pp. 5⅜ x 8½. 20070-1 Pa. $3.95

LIFE IN ANCIENT EGYPT, Adolf Erman. Fullest, most thorough, detailed older account with much not in more recent books, domestic life, religion, magic, medicine, commerce, much more. Many illustrations reproduce tomb paintings, carvings, hieroglyphs, etc. 597pp. 5⅜ x 8½. 22632-8 Pa. $12.95

SUNDIALS, Their Theory and Construction, Albert Waugh. Far and away the best, most thorough coverage of ideas, mathematics concerned, types, construction, adjusting anywhere. Simple, nontechnical treatment allows even children to build several of these dials. Over 100 illustrations. 230pp. 5⅜ x 8½. 22947-5 Pa. $8.95

THEORETICAL HYDRODYNAMICS, L. M. Milne-Thomson. Classic exposition of the mathematical theory of fluid motion, applicable to both hydrodynamics and aerodynamics. Over 600 exercises. 768pp. 6⅛ x 9¼. 68970-0 Pa. $20.95

SONGS OF EXPERIENCE: Facsimile Reproduction with 26 Plates in Full Color, William Blake. 26 full-color plates from a rare 1826 edition. Includes "TheTyger," "London," "Holy Thursday," and other poems. Printed text of poems. 48pp. 5¼ x 7. 24636-1 Pa. $4.95

OLD-TIME VIGNETTES IN FULL COLOR, Carol Belanger Grafton (ed.). Over 390 charming, often sentimental illustrations, selected from archives of Victorian graphics—pretty women posing, children playing, food, flowers, kittens and puppies, smiling cherubs, birds and butterflies, much more. All copyright-free. 48pp. 9¼ x 12¼. 27269-9 Pa. $9.95

PERSPECTIVE FOR ARTISTS, Rex Vicat Cole. Depth, perspective of sky and sea, shadows, much more, not usually covered. 391 diagrams, 81 reproductions of drawings and paintings. 279pp. 5⅜ x 8½. 22487-2 Pa. $9.95

DRAWING THE LIVING FIGURE, Joseph Sheppard. Innovative approach to artistic anatomy focuses on specifics of surface anatomy, rather than muscles and bones. Over 170 drawings of live models in front, back and side views, and in widely varying poses. Accompanying diagrams. 177 illustrations. Introduction. Index. 144pp. 8⅜ x11¼. 26723-7 Pa. $9.95

GOTHIC AND OLD ENGLISH ALPHABETS: 100 Complete Fonts, Dan X. Solo. Add power, elegance to posters, signs, other graphics with 100 stunning copyright-free alphabets: Blackstone, Dolbey, Germania, 97 more–including many lower-case, numerals, punctuation marks. 104pp. 8⅛ x 11. 24695-7 Pa. $9.95

HOW TO DO BEADWORK, Mary White. Fundamental book on craft from simple projects to five-bead chains and woven works. 106 illustrations. 142pp. 5⅜ x 8. 20697-1 Pa. $5.95

THE BOOK OF WOOD CARVING, Charles Marshall Sayers. Finest book for beginners discusses fundamentals and offers 34 designs. "Absolutely first rate . . . well thought out and well executed."–E. J. Tangerman. 118pp. 7¾ x 10⅝. 23654-4 Pa. $7.95

ILLUSTRATED CATALOG OF CIVIL WAR MILITARY GOODS: Union Army Weapons, Insignia, Uniform Accessories, and Other Equipment, Schuyler, Hartley, and Graham. Rare, profusely illustrated 1846 catalog includes Union Army uniform and dress regulations, arms and ammunition, coats, insignia, flags, swords, rifles, etc. 226 illustrations. 160pp. 9 x 12. 24939-5 Pa. $12.95

WOMEN'S FASHIONS OF THE EARLY 1900s: An Unabridged Republication of "New York Fashions, 1909," National Cloak & Suit Co. Rare catalog of mail-order fashions documents women's and children's clothing styles shortly after the turn of the century. Captions offer full descriptions, prices. Invaluable resource for fashion, costume historians. Approximately 725 illustrations. 128pp. 8⅜ x 11¼. 27276-1 Pa. $12.95

THE 1912 AND 1915 GUSTAV STICKLEY FURNITURE CATALOGS, Gustav Stickley. With over 200 detailed illustrations and descriptions, these two catalogs are essential reading and reference materials and identification guides for Stickley furniture. Captions cite materials, dimensions and prices. 112pp. 6½ x 9¼. 26676-1 Pa. $9.95

EARLY AMERICAN LOCOMOTIVES, John H. White, Jr. Finest locomotive engravings from early 19th century: historical (1804–74), main-line (after 1870), special, foreign, etc. 147 plates. 142pp. 11⅜ x 8¼. 22772-3 Pa. $12.95

THE TALL SHIPS OF TODAY IN PHOTOGRAPHS, Frank O. Braynard. Lavishly illustrated tribute to nearly 100 majestic contemporary sailing vessels: Amerigo Vespucci, Clearwater, Constitution, Eagle, Mayflower, Sea Cloud, Victory, many more. Authoritative captions provide statistics, background on each ship. 190 black-and-white photographs and illustrations. Introduction. 128pp. 8⅞ x 11¾. 27163-3 Pa. $14.95

LITTLE BOOK OF EARLY AMERICAN CRAFTS AND TRADES, Peter Stockham (ed.). 1807 children's book explains crafts and trades: baker, hatter, cooper, potter, and many others. 23 copperplate illustrations. 140pp. 4⅝ x 6.
23336-7 Pa. $4.95

VICTORIAN FASHIONS AND COSTUMES FROM HARPER'S BAZAR, 1867–1898, Stella Blum (ed.). Day costumes, evening wear, sports clothes, shoes, hats, other accessories in over 1,000 detailed engravings. 320pp. 9⅜ x 12¼.
22990-4 Pa. $16.95

GUSTAV STICKLEY, THE CRAFTSMAN, Mary Ann Smith. Superb study surveys broad scope of Stickley's achievement, especially in architecture. Design philosophy, rise and fall of the Craftsman empire, descriptions and floor plans for many Craftsman houses, more. 86 black-and-white halftones. 31 line illustrations. Introduction 208pp. 6½ x 9¼. 27210-9 Pa. $9.95

THE LONG ISLAND RAIL ROAD IN EARLY PHOTOGRAPHS, Ron Ziel. Over 220 rare photos, informative text document origin (1844) and development of rail service on Long Island. Vintage views of early trains, locomotives, stations, passengers, crews, much more. Captions. 8⅞ x 11¾. 26301-0 Pa. $14.95

VOYAGE OF THE LIBERDADE, Joshua Slocum. Great 19th-century mariner's thrilling, first-hand account of the wreck of his ship off South America, the 35-foot boat he built from the wreckage, and its remarkable voyage home. 128pp. 5⅜ x 8½.
40022-0 Pa. $5.95

TEN BOOKS ON ARCHITECTURE, Vitruvius. The most important book ever written on architecture. Early Roman aesthetics, technology, classical orders, site selection, all other aspects. Morgan translation. 331pp. 5⅜ x 8½. 20645-9 Pa. $9.95

THE HUMAN FIGURE IN MOTION, Eadweard Muybridge. More than 4,500 stopped-action photos, in action series, showing undraped men, women, children jumping, lying down, throwing, sitting, wrestling, carrying, etc. 390pp. 7⅞ x 10⅝.
20204-6 Clothbd. $29.95

TREES OF THE EASTERN AND CENTRAL UNITED STATES AND CANADA, William M. Harlow. Best one-volume guide to 140 trees. Full descriptions, woodlore, range, etc. Over 600 illustrations. Handy size. 288pp. 4½ x 6⅜.
20395-6 Pa. $6.95

SONGS OF WESTERN BIRDS, Dr. Donald J. Borror. Complete song and call repertoire of 60 western species, including flycatchers, juncoes, cactus wrens, many more–includes fully illustrated booklet. Cassette and manual 99913-0 $8.95

GROWING AND USING HERBS AND SPICES, Milo Miloradovich. Versatile handbook provides all the information needed for cultivation and use of all the herbs and spices available in North America. 4 illustrations. Index. Glossary. 236pp. 5⅜ x 8½.
25058-X Pa. $7.95

BIG BOOK OF MAZES AND LABYRINTHS, Walter Shepherd. 50 mazes and labyrinths in all–classical, solid, ripple, and more–in one great volume. Perfect inexpensive puzzler for clever youngsters. Full solutions. 112pp. 8⅛ x 11.
22951-3 Pa. $5.95

PIANO TUNING, J. Cree Fischer. Clearest, best book for beginner, amateur. Simple repairs, raising dropped notes, tuning by easy method of flattened fifths. No previous skills needed. 4 illustrations. 201pp. 5⅜ x 8½. 23267-0 Pa. $6.95

HINTS TO SINGERS, Lillian Nordica. Selecting the right teacher, developing confidence, overcoming stage fright, and many other important skills receive thoughtful discussion in this indispensible guide, written by a world-famous diva of four decades' experience. 96pp. 5⅜ x 8½. 40094-8 Pa. $4.95

THE COMPLETE NONSENSE OF EDWARD LEAR, Edward Lear. All nonsense limericks, zany alphabets, Owl and Pussycat, songs, nonsense botany, etc., illustrated by Lear. Total of 320pp. 5⅜ x 8½. (Available in U.S. only.) 20167-8 Pa. $7.95

VICTORIAN PARLOUR POETRY: An Annotated Anthology, Michael R. Turner. 117 gems by Longfellow, Tennyson, Browning, many lesser-known poets. "The Village Blacksmith," "Curfew Must Not Ring Tonight," "Only a Baby Small," dozens more, often difficult to find elsewhere. Index of poets, titles, first lines. xxiii + 325pp. 5⅝ x 8¼. 27044-0 Pa. $12.95

DUBLINERS, James Joyce. Fifteen stories offer vivid, tightly focused observations of the lives of Dublin's poorer classes. At least one, "The Dead," is considered a masterpiece. Reprinted complete and unabridged from standard edition. 160pp. 5 3/16 x 8¼. 26870-5 Pa. $1.50

GREAT WEIRD TALES: 14 Stories by Lovecraft, Blackwood, Machen and Others, S. T. Joshi (ed.). 14 spellbinding tales, including "The Sin Eater," by Fiona McLeod, "The Eye Above the Mantel," by Frank Belknap Long, as well as renowned works by R. H. Barlow, Lord Dunsany, Arthur Machen, W. C. Morrow and eight other masters of the genre. 256pp. 5⅜ x 8½. (Available in U.S. only.) 40436-6 Pa. $8.95

THE BOOK OF THE SACRED MAGIC OF ABRAMELIN THE MAGE, translated by S. MacGregor Mathers. Medieval manuscript of ceremonial magic. Basic document in Aleister Crowley, Golden Dawn groups. 268pp. 5⅜ x 8½. 23211-5 Pa. $9.95

NEW RUSSIAN-ENGLISH AND ENGLISH-RUSSIAN DICTIONARY, M. A. O'Brien. This is a remarkably handy Russian dictionary, containing a surprising amount of information, including over 70,000 entries. 366pp. 4½ x 6⅛. 20208-9 Pa. $10.95

HISTORIC HOMES OF THE AMERICAN PRESIDENTS, Second, Revised Edition, Irvin Haas. A traveler's guide to American Presidential homes, most open to the public, depicting and describing homes occupied by every American President from George Washington to George Bush. With visiting hours, admission charges, travel routes. 175 photographs. Index. 160pp. 8¼ x 11. 26751-2 Pa. $13.95

NEW YORK IN THE FORTIES, Andreas Feininger. 162 brilliant photographs by the well-known photographer, formerly with *Life* magazine. Commuters, shoppers, Times Square at night, much else from city at its peak. Captions by John von Hartz. 181pp. 9¼ x 10¾. 23585-8 Pa. $13.95

INDIAN SIGN LANGUAGE, William Tomkins. Over 525 signs developed by Sioux and other tribes. Written instructions and diagrams. Also 290 pictographs. 111pp. 6⅛ x 9¼. 22029-X Pa. $3.95

CATALOG OF DOVER BOOKS

ANATOMY: A Complete Guide for Artists, Joseph Sheppard. A master of figure drawing shows artists how to render human anatomy convincingly. Over 460 illustrations. 224pp. 8⅜ x 11¼. 27279-6 Pa. $11.95

MEDIEVAL CALLIGRAPHY: Its History and Technique, Marc Drogin. Spirited history, comprehensive instruction manual covers 13 styles (ca. 4th century through 15th). Excellent photographs; directions for duplicating medieval techniques with modern tools. 224pp. 8⅜ x 11¼. 26142-5 Pa. $12.95

DRIED FLOWERS: How to Prepare Them, Sarah Whitlock and Martha Rankin. Complete instructions on how to use silica gel, meal and borax, perlite aggregate, sand and borax, glycerine and water to create attractive permanent flower arrangements. 12 illustrations. 32pp. 5⅜ x 8½. 21802-3 Pa. $1.00

EASY-TO-MAKE BIRD FEEDERS FOR WOODWORKERS, Scott D. Campbell. Detailed, simple-to-use guide for designing, constructing, caring for and using feeders. Text, illustrations for 12 classic and contemporary designs. 96pp. 5⅜ x 8½. 25847-5 Pa. $3.95

SCOTTISH WONDER TALES FROM MYTH AND LEGEND, Donald A. Mackenzie. 16 lively tales tell of giants rumbling down mountainsides, of a magic wand that turns stone pillars into warriors, of gods and goddesses, evil hags, powerful forces and more. 240pp. 5⅜ x 8½. 29677-6 Pa. $6.95

THE HISTORY OF UNDERCLOTHES, C. Willett Cunnington and Phyllis Cunnington. Fascinating, well-documented survey covering six centuries of English undergarments, enhanced with over 100 illustrations: 12th-century laced-up bodice, footed long drawers (1795), 19th-century bustles, 19th-century corsets for men, Victorian "bust improvers," much more. 272pp. 5⅝ x 8¼. 27124-2 Pa. $9.95

ARTS AND CRAFTS FURNITURE: The Complete Brooks Catalog of 1912, Brooks Manufacturing Co. Photos and detailed descriptions of more than 150 now very collectible furniture designs from the Arts and Crafts movement depict davenports, settees, buffets, desks, tables, chairs, bedsteads, dressers and more, all built of solid, quarter-sawed oak. Invaluable for students and enthusiasts of antiques, Americana and the decorative arts. 80pp. 6½ x 9¼. 27471-3 Pa. $8.95

WILBUR AND ORVILLE: A Biography of the Wright Brothers, Fred Howard. Definitive, crisply written study tells the full story of the brothers' lives and work. A vividly written biography, unparalleled in scope and color, that also captures the spirit of an extraordinary era. 560pp. 6⅛ x 9¼. 40297-5 Pa. $17.95

THE ARTS OF THE SAILOR: Knotting, Splicing and Ropework, Hervey Garrett Smith. Indispensable shipboard reference covers tools, basic knots and useful hitches; handsewing and canvas work, more. Over 100 illustrations. Delightful reading for sea lovers. 256pp. 5⅜ x 8½. 26440-8 Pa. $8.95

FRANK LLOYD WRIGHT'S FALLINGWATER: The House and Its History, Second, Revised Edition, Donald Hoffmann. A total revision–both in text and illustrations–of the standard document on Fallingwater, the boldest, most personal architectural statement of Wright's mature years, updated with valuable new material from the recently opened Frank Lloyd Wright Archives. "Fascinating"–*The New York Times*. 116 illustrations. 128pp. 9¼ x 10¾. 27430-6 Pa. $12.95

PHOTOGRAPHIC SKETCHBOOK OF THE CIVIL WAR, Alexander Gardner. 100 photos taken on field during the Civil War. Famous shots of Manassas Harper's Ferry, Lincoln, Richmond, slave pens, etc. 244pp. 10⅝ x 8¼. 22731-6 Pa. $10.95

FIVE ACRES AND INDEPENDENCE, Maurice G. Kains. Great back-to-the-land classic explains basics of self-sufficient farming. The one book to get. 95 illustrations. 397pp. 5⅜ x 8½. 20974-1 Pa. $7.95

SONGS OF EASTERN BIRDS, Dr. Donald J. Borror. Songs and calls of 60 species most common to eastern U.S.: warblers, woodpeckers, flycatchers, thrushes, larks, many more in high-quality recording. Cassette and manual 99912-2 $9.95

A MODERN HERBAL, Margaret Grieve. Much the fullest, most exact, most useful compilation of herbal material. Gigantic alphabetical encyclopedia, from aconite to zedoary, gives botanical information, medical properties, folklore, economic uses, much else. Indispensable to serious reader. 161 illustrations. 888pp. 6½ x 9¼. 2-vol. set. (Available in U.S. only.) Vol. I: 22798-7 Pa. $10.95
Vol. II: 22799-5 Pa. $10.95

HIDDEN TREASURE MAZE BOOK, Dave Phillips. Solve 34 challenging mazes accompanied by heroic tales of adventure. Evil dragons, people-eating plants, bloodthirsty giants, many more dangerous adversaries lurk at every twist and turn. 34 mazes, stories, solutions. 48pp. 8¼ x 11. 24566-7 Pa. $2.95

LETTERS OF W. A. MOZART, Wolfgang A. Mozart. Remarkable letters show bawdy wit, humor, imagination, musical insights, contemporary musical world; includes some letters from Leopold Mozart. 276pp. 5⅜ x 8½. 22859-2 Pa. $9.95

BASIC PRINCIPLES OF CLASSICAL BALLET, Agrippina Vaganova. Great Russian theoretician, teacher explains methods for teaching classical ballet. 118 illustrations. 175pp. 5⅜ x 8½. 22036-2 Pa. $6.95

THE JUMPING FROG, Mark Twain. Revenge edition. The original story of The Celebrated Jumping Frog of Calaveras County, a hapless French translation, and Twain's hilarious "retranslation" from the French. 12 illustrations. 66pp. 5⅜ x 8½.
22686-7 Pa. $4.95

BEST REMEMBERED POEMS, Martin Gardner (ed.). The 126 poems in this superb collection of 19th- and 20th-century British and American verse range from Shelley's "To a Skylark" to the impassioned "Renascence" of Edna St. Vincent Millay and to Edward Lear's whimsical "The Owl and the Pussycat." 224pp. 5⅜ x 8½.
27165-X Pa. $5.95

COMPLETE SONNETS, William Shakespeare. Over 150 exquisite poems deal with love, friendship, the tyranny of time, beauty's evanescence, death and other themes in language of remarkable power, precision and beauty. Glossary of archaic terms. 80pp. 5$\frac{3}{16}$ x 8¼. 26686-9 Pa. $1.00

THE BATTLES THAT CHANGED HISTORY, Fletcher Pratt. Eminent historian profiles 16 crucial conflicts, ancient to modern, that changed the course of civilization. 352pp. 5⅜ x 8½. 41129-X Pa. $9.95

THE WIT AND HUMOR OF OSCAR WILDE, Alvin Redman (ed.). More than 1,000 ripostes, paradoxes, wisecracks: Work is the curse of the drinking classes; I can resist everything except temptation; etc. 258pp. 5⅜ x 8½. 20602-5 Pa. $6.95

SHAKESPEARE LEXICON AND QUOTATION DICTIONARY, Alexander Schmidt. Full definitions, locations, shades of meaning in every word in plays and poems. More than 50,000 exact quotations. 1,485pp. 6½ x 9¼. 2-vol. set.
Vol. 1: 22726-X Pa. $17.95
Vol. 2: 22727-8 Pa. $17.95

SELECTED POEMS, Emily Dickinson. Over 100 best-known, best-loved poems by one of America's foremost poets, reprinted from authoritative early editions. No comparable edition at this price. Index of first lines. 64pp. 5$\frac{3}{16}$ x 8¼. 26466-1 Pa. $1.00

THE INSIDIOUS DR. FU-MANCHU, Sax Rohmer. The first of the popular mystery series introduces a pair of English detectives to their archnemesis, the diabolical Dr. Fu-Manchu. Flavorful atmosphere, fast-paced action, and colorful characters enliven this classic of the genre. 208pp. 5$\frac{3}{16}$ x 8¼. 29898-1 Pa. $2.00

THE MALLEUS MALEFICARUM OF KRAMER AND SPRENGER, translated by Montague Summers. Full text of most important witchhunter's "bible," used by both Catholics and Protestants. 278pp. 6⅝ x 10. 22802-9 Pa. $12.95

SPANISH STORIES/CUENTOS ESPAÑOLES: A Dual-Language Book, Angel Flores (ed.). Unique format offers 13 great stories in Spanish by Cervantes, Borges, others. Faithful English translations on facing pages. 352pp. 5⅜ x 8½. 25399-6 Pa. $9.95

GARDEN CITY, LONG ISLAND, IN EARLY PHOTOGRAPHS, 1869–1919, Mildred H. Smith. Handsome treasury of 118 vintage pictures, accompanied by carefully researched captions, document the Garden City Hotel fire (1899), the Vanderbilt Cup Race (1908), the first airmail flight departing from the Nassau Boulevard Aerodrome (1911), and much more. 96pp. 8⅞ x 11¾. 40669-5 Pa. $12.95

OLD QUEENS, N.Y., IN EARLY PHOTOGRAPHS, Vincent F. Seyfried and William Asadorian. Over 160 rare photographs of Maspeth, Jamaica, Jackson Heights, and other areas. Vintage views of DeWitt Clinton mansion, 1939 World's Fair and more. Captions. 192pp. 8⅞ x 11. 26358-4 Pa. $14.95

CAPTURED BY THE INDIANS: 15 Firsthand Accounts, 1750-1870, Frederick Drimmer. Astounding true historical accounts of grisly torture, bloody conflicts, relentless pursuits, miraculous escapes and more, by people who lived to tell the tale. 384pp. 5⅜ x 8½. 24901-8 Pa. $9.95

THE WORLD'S GREAT SPEECHES (Fourth Enlarged Edition), Lewis Copeland, Lawrence W. Lamm, and Stephen J. McKenna. Nearly 300 speeches provide public speakers with a wealth of updated quotes and inspiration–from Pericles' funeral oration and William Jennings Bryan's "Cross of Gold Speech" to Malcolm X's powerful words on the Black Revolution and Earl of Spenser's tribute to his sister, Diana, Princess of Wales. 944pp. 5⅜ x 8⅜. 40903-1 Pa. $15.95

THE BOOK OF THE SWORD, Sir Richard F. Burton. Great Victorian scholar/adventurer's eloquent, erudite history of the "queen of weapons"–from prehistory to early Roman Empire. Evolution and development of early swords, variations (sabre, broadsword, cutlass, scimitar, etc.), much more. 336pp. 6⅛ x 9¼. 25434-8 Pa. $9.95

AUTOBIOGRAPHY: The Story of My Experiments with Truth, Mohandas K. Gandhi. Boyhood, legal studies, purification, the growth of the Satyagraha (nonviolent protest) movement. Critical, inspiring work of the man responsible for the freedom of India. 480pp. 5⅜ x 8½. (Available in U.S. only.) 24593-4 Pa. $9.95

CELTIC MYTHS AND LEGENDS, T. W. Rolleston. Masterful retelling of Irish and Welsh stories and tales. Cuchulain, King Arthur, Deirdre, the Grail, many more. First paperback edition. 58 full-page illustrations. 512pp. 5⅜ x 8½. 26507-2 Pa. $9.95

THE PRINCIPLES OF PSYCHOLOGY, William James. Famous long course complete, unabridged. Stream of thought, time perception, memory, experimental methods; great work decades ahead of its time. 94 figures. 1,391pp. 5⅜ x 8½. 2-vol. set.
Vol. I: 20381-6 Pa. $14.95
Vol. II: 20382-4 Pa. $16.95

THE WORLD AS WILL AND REPRESENTATION, Arthur Schopenhauer. Definitive English translation of Schopenhauer's life work, correcting more than 1,000 errors, omissions in earlier translations. Translated by E. F. J. Payne. Total of 1,269pp. 5⅜ x 8½. 2-vol. set.
Vol. 1: 21761-2 Pa. $12.95
Vol. 2: 21762-0 Pa. $12.95

MAGIC AND MYSTERY IN TIBET, Madame Alexandra David-Neel. Experiences among lamas, magicians, sages, sorcerers, Bonpa wizards. A true psychic discovery. 32 illustrations. 321pp. 5⅜ x 8½. (Available in U.S. only.) 22682-4 Pa. $9.95

THE EGYPTIAN BOOK OF THE DEAD, E. A. Wallis Budge. Complete reproduction of Ani's papyrus, finest ever found. Full hieroglyphic text, interlinear transliteration, word-for-word translation, smooth translation. 533pp. 6½ x 9¼.
21866-X Pa. $12.95

MATHEMATICS FOR THE NONMATHEMATICIAN, Morris Kline. Detailed, college-level treatment of mathematics in cultural and historical context, with numerous exercises. Recommended Reading Lists. Tables. Numerous figures. 641pp. 5⅜ x 8½.
24823-2 Pa. $11.95

PROBABILISTIC METHODS IN THE THEORY OF STRUCTURES, Isaac Elishakoff. Well-written introduction covers the elements of the theory of probability from two or more random variables, the reliability of such multivariable structures, the theory of random function, Monte Carlo methods of treating problems incapable of exact solution, and more. Examples. 502pp. 5³/₈ x 8¹/₂. 40691-1 Pa. $16.95

THE RIME OF THE ANCIENT MARINER, Gustave Doré, S. T. Coleridge. Doré's finest work; 34 plates capture moods, subtleties of poem. Flawless full-size reproductions printed on facing pages with authoritative text of poem. "Beautiful. Simply beautiful."–*Publisher's Weekly.* 77pp. 9¼ x 12. 22305-1 Pa. $7.95

NORTH AMERICAN INDIAN DESIGNS FOR ARTISTS AND CRAFTSPEOPLE, Eva Wilson. Over 360 authentic copyright-free designs adapted from Navajo blankets, Hopi pottery, Sioux buffalo hides, more. Geometrics, symbolic figures, plant and animal motifs, etc. 128pp. 8⅜ x 11. (Not for sale in the United Kingdom.) 25341-4 Pa. $9.95

SCULPTURE: Principles and Practice, Louis Slobodkin. Step-by-step approach to clay, plaster, metals, stone; classical and modern. 253 drawings, photos. 255pp. 8⅛ x 11.
22960-2 Pa. $11.95

THE INFLUENCE OF SEA POWER UPON HISTORY, 1660–1783, A. T. Mahan. Influential classic of naval history and tactics still used as text in war colleges. First paperback edition. 4 maps. 24 battle plans. 640pp. 5⅜ x 8½.   25509-3 Pa. $14.95

THE STORY OF THE TITANIC AS TOLD BY ITS SURVIVORS, Jack Winocour (ed.). What it was really like. Panic, despair, shocking inefficiency, and a little heroism. More thrilling than any fictional account. 26 illustrations. 320pp. 5⅜ x 8½.
20610-6 Pa. $8.95

FAIRY AND FOLK TALES OF THE IRISH PEASANTRY, William Butler Yeats (ed.). Treasury of 64 tales from the twilight world of Celtic myth and legend: "The Soul Cages," "The Kildare Pooka," "King O'Toole and his Goose," many more. Introduction and Notes by W. B. Yeats. 352pp. 5⅜ x 8½.   26941-8 Pa. $8.95

BUDDHIST MAHAYANA TEXTS, E. B. Cowell and others (eds.). Superb, accurate translations of basic documents in Mahayana Buddhism, highly important in history of religions. The Buddha-karita of Asvaghosha, Larger Sukhavativyuha, more. 448pp. 5⅜ x 8½.   25552-2 Pa. $12.95

ONE TWO THREE . . . INFINITY: Facts and Speculations of Science, George Gamow. Great physicist's fascinating, readable overview of contemporary science: number theory, relativity, fourth dimension, entropy, genes, atomic structure, much more. 128 illustrations. Index. 352pp. 5⅜ x 8½.   25664-2 Pa. $9.95

EXPERIMENTATION AND MEASUREMENT, W. J. Youden. Introductory manual explains laws of measurement in simple terms and offers tips for achieving accuracy and minimizing errors. Mathematics of measurement, use of instruments, experimenting with machines. 1994 edition. Foreword. Preface. Introduction. Epilogue. Selected Readings. Glossary. Index. Tables and figures. 128pp. 5³/₈ x 8¹/₂.
40451-X Pa. $6.95

DALÍ ON MODERN ART: The Cuckolds of Antiquated Modern Art, Salvador Dalí. Influential painter skewers modern art and its practitioners. Outrageous evaluations of Picasso, Cézanne, Turner, more. 15 renderings of paintings discussed. 44 calligraphic decorations by Dalí. 96pp. 5⅜ x 8½. (Available in U.S. only.)   29220-7 Pa. $5.95

ANTIQUE PLAYING CARDS: A Pictorial History, Henry René D'Allemagne. Over 900 elaborate, decorative images from rare playing cards (14th–20th centuries): Bacchus, death, dancing dogs, hunting scenes, royal coats of arms, players cheating, much more. 96pp. 9¼ x 12¼.   29265-7 Pa. $12.95

MAKING FURNITURE MASTERPIECES: 30 Projects with Measured Drawings, Franklin H. Gottshall. Step-by-step instructions, illustrations for constructing handsome, useful pieces, among them a Sheraton desk, Chippendale chair, Spanish desk, Queen Anne table and a William and Mary dressing mirror. 224pp. 8⅛ x 11¼.
29338-6 Pa. $16.95

THE FOSSIL BOOK: A Record of Prehistoric Life, Patricia V. Rich et al. Profusely illustrated definitive guide covers everything from single-celled organisms and dinosaurs to birds and mammals and the interplay between climate and man. Over 1,500 illustrations. 760pp. 7½ x 10⅛.   29371-8 Pa. $29.95

Prices subject to change without notice.

Available at your book dealer or write for free catalog to Dept. GI, Dover Publications, Inc., 31 East 2nd St., Mineola, N.Y. 11501. Dover publishes more than 500 books each year on science, elementary and advanced mathematics, biology, music, art, literary history, social sciences and other areas.